Gold'n Delicious

Recipes hand-picked from the Great Northwest

The Junior League of Spokane

The Junior League of Spokane is an organization of women committed to promoting voluntarism and to improving the community through the effective action and leadership of trained volunteers. Its purpose is exclusively educational and charitable.

The Junior League of Spokane reaches out to women of all races, religions and national origins who demonstrate an interest in and commitment to voluntarism.

Photography: Barros & Barros
Concept and Design: Robideaux Warner
Copy: Candace Dahlstrom and Toni Robideaux
Food Styling: Stephanie Puddy
Prop Styling: Leslie Warner and Stephanie Puddy
Printed on recycled paper in the USA by Lawton Printing
Published in the USA by The Junior League of Spokane
First Printing, October 1995, 15,000 copies
Second Printing, May 1996, 20,000 copies

Additional copies of GOLD'n Delicious may be obtained from:
The Junior League of Spokane
910 North Washington, Suite 228
Spokane, WA 99201-2260
Phone (509) 328-2166
Fax (509) 328-1827

If you are concerned about bacterial problems associated with raw eggs, certain recipes should be avoided or modified. Special consideration should be given to infants, the ill and the elderly.

Cover photo: Salmon en Papillote, Washington Wild Rice and Marinated Asparagus

We invite you to bask in the golden glow of entertaining family and friends with this treasury of recipes hand-picked, hand-tested and handed down by The Junior League of Spokane.

This collection embraces the land we live in...the distinct flavors of the seasons, the incomparable natural beauty of the northwest and a rich harvest of tantalizing local fare. Welcome to a land where the outdoors is our passion. We hike, bike and ski on the wooded mountain trails and are renewed by the bountiful lakes and streams. The arrival of each new season is warmly anticipated for its unique pleasures.

While this natural setting defines and enriches our lives, it is the deeply-felt sense of community and cherished family traditions which keep us warm on cold winter nights. Therein lies our real treasure. These recipes celebrate the gold of community and the delicious warmth of a gathering. As with all great food, the joy is in the sharing.

It's a heart you can trust! The Junior League of Spokane believes lowering fat in food doesn't need to compromise flavor. To help us certify recipes as low-fat we partnered with The Heart Institute of Spokane, a non-profit organization dedicated to cardiac care, education and research.

When you see The Institute's Lite 'n Hearty symbol   you're assured the recipe was analyzed by a registered dietitian, obtains fewer than 30% of its calories from fat and will truly taste...GOLD'n Delicious

---

The Junior League of Spokane thanks

its corporate sponsors who have contributed to this book.
We appreciate their continuing support.

Category Sponsors

Great Harvest Bread Co.
Sterling Savings Association
Washington Trust Bank

Menu Sponsor

Wendle Ford

Props

Fitness Fanatics
Joel Inc.
Mel's
Nordstrom

TABLE OF CONTENTS

MENUS
6

APPETIZERS & BEVERAGES
10

BREADS & BREAKFAST
40

SOUPS
66

SALADS
78

PASTAS
102

FISH & SEAFOOD
120

POULTRY
138

MEATS
158

VEGETABLES & SIDE DISHES
178

DESSERTS
202

INDEX
232

Spring

*Spokane shapes up each spring with its
inspiring city-wide Bloomsday Run.*

*Fragrant purple and white lilacs burst
on the scene in May and give Spokane
its nickname of the Lilac City.*

Carbo-Load Bloomsday™ Dinner

In celebration of a crazy notion that a whole
community could become healthier together,
Spokane hosts the largest timed foot race in
the world...Bloomsday. This surprisingly low-
fat meal is guaranteed to give runners an
energy boost midway up Doomsday Hill.

Hearty Lasagna
page 118

Italian Breadsticks
page 53

Spinach Salad with Papaya Salsa
page 96

Surprise Packages
page 220

Mother's Day Lilac Brunch

Spring holds infinite promise of new
beginnings. Start a tradition with this make-
ahead Sunday brunch. It's so easy
you'll even have time to visit with guests,
so scrumptious there won't be any
leftovers...but please don't eat the lilacs!

Golden Cooler
page 38

No Guilt Strata
page 64

Springtime Salad
page 93

Cream Cheese Crescents
page 45

Pecan Mini-Muffins
page 43

Summer

*Sailboats flourish on glittering
Lake Coeur d'Alene.*

*Catch the brass ring on the historic hand-
carved Looff Carrousel in Riverfront Park.*

Easy Sailing Appetizers

It wouldn't be summer without a cruise on
the lake. If you don't have a sailboat, then
commandeer anything that floats. These
delicious appetizers have been tested on
captains and crews from Priest Lake
to Lake Coeur d'Alene.

Bleu Ribbon Dip
page 30

Joanne's Spicy Shrimp Salsa
page 28

Confetti Relish
page 32

Fabulous Fruit Dip
page 36

Carrousel Birthday Party

Merry-go-rounds and birthday parties bring out
the kid in all of us. This menu made the
rounds of our young taste testers and passed
with flying colors. Try these kid-pleasers at a
picnic in the park or any backyard festivity.

Picnic Pizza Bread
page 57

Favorite Fruit
page 93

Carrots for Kids
page 196

Chocolate Marble Cake
page 206

Autumn

The sun-drenched wheat fields of the rich Palouse herald the beginning of harvest.

The Centennial Trail is a corridor of spectacular beauty that weaves its way along the Spokane River.

Harvest Moon Celebration

The air holds a promise of cooler weather and it's time to pull out the sweaters and pull up the last of the carrots from the garden. A kitchen warmed by good friends, a simmering stew and fresh-baked harvest bread create memories of pure gold. The centerpiece – a sheaf of wheat and the last rose before the frost.

Brandied Beef Stew
page 168

Herbed Green Beans with Pine Nuts
page 199

Autumn Salad with Spicy Walnuts
page 99

Golden Harvest Bread
page 52

Autumn on the Trail

Call your best friends, hoist the bikes on the rack, pack the kids in the back and you're off to explore the great outdoors. Don't settle for hard tack and biscuits. Pioneer a picnic tradition of your own with this easy gourmet traveling feast.

Spicy Steak and Pasta Salad with Shiitake Mushrooms
page 81

Swiss Onion Bread Ring
page 55

Marinated Asparagus
page 191

Not-Your-Average Chocolate Chip Cookie
page 224

MENUS

Winter

Schweitzer Ski Resort, with its breathtaking view of the Rockies, provides world-class family fun.

The Opera House is the perfect setting for an elegant evening on the town.

APRÈS SKI WARM-UP

The reward for a day spent challenging the slopes? A gathering of good friends to warm your heart, a crackling fire to warm your toes and the best chili north of the border to warm your insides.

Robin's Chunky Chili
page 167

Focaccia Bread with Brie and Sun-Dried Tomatoes
page 61

The Ultimate Endive Salad
page 98

Babe Ruth Bars
page 227

SYMPHONY DESSERT BUFFET

After an evening of Vivaldi or Gershwin, indulge your appetite for elegance with a symphony of desserts...mellow and rich like the golden tones of a french horn. Music may soothe the soul but there's nothing so satisfying as chocolate and friendship.

Iced Spiked Coffee
page 39

Peppy Pecans
page 36

Chocolate Macadamia Tart
page 216

Northwest Huckleberry Pie
page 214

Amaretto and Chocolate Chip Cheesecake
page 211

APPETIZERS & BEVERAGES

Smoked Salmon with Apples
12

Salmon Tartlets
13

Citrus-Sauced Crab Cakes
14

Seafood Pepper Strips
15

Shrimp and Tortellini Kabobs
16

Glazed Shrimp Kabobs
17

Layered Tomato Pesto
17

Steamed Clams with Sherry and Herbs
18

Phyllo-Wrapped Brie with Red Pepper Jelly
19

Red Pepper Jelly
19

Walla Walla Sweet Squares
20

Frosted Spinach Torte
21

Spinach and Feta Mushroom Caps
22

Mediterranean Skewers
23

Lamb and Melon Kabobs
24

Korean Beef
25

Smoked Turkey in Endive
26

Party Bread
27

Roasted Red Pepper Crostini
28

Joanne's Spicy Shrimp Salsa
28

Black Bean Salsa
29

Dill Dip with a Twist
30

Bleu Ribbon Dip
30

Rave Reviews Dip
31

Garden Herb Cheese Spread
31

Confetti Relish
32

Artichoke Relish with Pita Chips
33

Best-of-the-Best Artichoke Dip
34

Fontina Quesadillas
34

Blind Date Dip
35

Fabulous Fruit Dip
36

Peppy Pecans
36

Apple Cider Surprise
37

Cranberry Tea
37

Golden Cooler
38

Conrad's Gin Fizz
38

Bull's Eye Bloody Mary
39

Iced Spiked Coffee
39

Photo: Smoked Salmon with Apples, Shrimp and Tortellini Kabobs, Dill Dip with a Twist and Bull's Eye Bloody Mary

Smoked Salmon with Apples

1/4 cup unsalted butter, softened

12 slices thin, firm-textured white bread, crusts removed

4 tablespoons fresh dill, chopped and divided

2 to 3 Red Delicious apples, divided

2 1/2 tablespoons lemon juice, divided

2 tablespoons mayonnaise

4 teaspoons prepared horseradish, drained

2 tablespoons red onion, minced

1 tablespoon parsley, minced

1/4 teaspoon salt

1/8 teaspoon freshly ground black pepper

16 ounces smoked salmon, skinned and cut into 1/2-inch pieces

dill sprigs for garnish, optional

Butter one side of each piece of bread and sprinkle the slices with 3 tablespoons dill. Cut each slice into 4 triangles. Broil, buttered side up, until lightly browned. Turn off broiler, flip triangles and let rest in oven until dry and crisp, about 10 minutes. Transfer to a rack and cool.

Core and mince half of one apple. Toss with 1/2 tablespoon lemon juice. Combine minced apple with remaining 1 tablespoon dill, mayonnaise, horseradish, onion, parsley, salt and pepper.

Remove core from remaining apples and slice into 48 1/4-inch pieces. Toss with remaining 2 tablespoons lemon juice. Pat apple slices dry and place one on each toast triangle. Top with 1 teaspoon of the minced apple mixture followed by a piece of salmon. Garnish each with a small sprig of dill, if desired.

Makes 48

Salmon Tartlets

Tartlet Shells

 1 large egg white

 2 tablespoons olive oil

 1/4 teaspoon salt

 8 (12 x 16-inch) sheets
   phyllo dough, thawed

   vegetable cooking spray

Smoked Salmon Filling

 2 (8-ounce) packages cream
   cheese

 8 ounces smoked salmon fillets,
   skin and bones removed

 2 green onions, sliced

 4 teaspoons horseradish,
   drained

Garnish

 1 cup cucumber, shredded

For the tartlet shells, whisk together egg white, oil and salt in a small bowl. Lay one sheet of phyllo on work surface and lightly brush it with the egg white mixture. Lay a second phyllo sheet on top of the first and brush again. Repeat with the third sheet. Top with the fourth sheet of phyllo, but do not brush with egg white mixture. Follow the instructions on the packaged phyllo dough to keep the remaining sheets from drying out.

Cut layered dough into 4 lengthwise strips and 6 crosswise strips for a total of 24 pieces. Lightly coat 2 mini-muffin pans with vegetable cooking spray. Press pieces into muffin cups and bake at 325° for 8 to 12 minutes or until golden and crisp. Cool on a rack. Repeat procedure with remaining phyllo and egg white mixture. (Tartlets can be stored in a closed container at room temperature for up to one week or frozen for 2 months.)

For the salmon filling, combine cream cheese and smoked salmon in a food processor. Process until fairly smooth. Add onions and horseradish and pulse until just combined. (Filling can be made ahead and refrigerated for up to 2 days.)

To assemble, spoon 1 heaping teaspoon of filling into each tartlet shell and garnish with shredded cucumber.

Makes 48

Citrus-Sauced Crab Cakes

Sauce

1 1/2 **cups pink grapefruit juice**

3/4 **cup dry white wine**

3/4 **cup shallots,
(about 6 large) sliced**

15 **whole peppercorns**

1/2 **cup butter**

Crab Cakes

3/4 **pound fresh crabmeat**

1/4 **cup celery, minced**

1/4 **cup red onion, minced**

3 **tablespoons light mayonnaise**

1 **egg, beaten to blend**

2 **tablespoons mild green chilies,
diced**

1 **teaspoon Worcestershire sauce**

3 **cups fresh bread crumbs,
divided**

2 **tablespoons butter**

Combine grapefruit juice, wine, shallots and peppercorns in a skillet. Bring to a boil and cook until liquid is reduced to 3 tablespoons, about 20 minutes. Strain. (Can be done 1 day ahead. Cover and refrigerate.)

Combine crabmeat, celery, onion, mayonnaise, egg, chilies, Worcestershire and 1 cup of bread crumbs in a bowl. Divide into eight mounds. Flatten each crab cake to a 3/4-inch thick patty. Place remaining 2 cups bread crumbs on a plate and coat each patty with bread crumbs. (Can be made 2 hours ahead. Cover and chill.)

Melt 2 tablespoons butter in a large, heavy skillet over medium heat. Add crab cakes in batches. Cook until golden brown, about 4 minutes per side. Transfer to baking sheet and keep warm in oven.

Bring grapefruit sauce to simmer in a medium, heavy saucepan. Reduce heat to low and add 1/2 cup butter, whisking until melted. Transfer crab cakes to plates. Drizzle with sauce and serve.

Serves 8

These crab cakes are also delicious when made with imitation crab!

Seafood Pepper Strips

Filling

- 1/2 **pound fresh lump crabmeat, cartilage removed**
- 1/3 **cup mayonnaise**
- 2 **green onions, finely chopped**
- 1/2 **plum tomato, seeded and minced**
- 1 **teaspoon dried parsley**
- 1 **teaspoon dried tarragon**
- 2 **teaspoons lemon juice**
- 1/2 **teaspoon grated lemon peel**
- 1/8 **teaspoon cayenne pepper**

Pepper Strips

- 2 **red, yellow or green bell peppers, cut into 1 x 2-inch strips**

Combine filling ingredients and mix well. Cover and refrigerate for 1 to 24 hours.

Spoon 1 to 2 teaspoons filling onto each pepper strip. Arrange on a serving platter. Serve immediately or cover and refrigerate for up to 3 hours.

Serves 6 to 8

Soak onion rings in beet juice to make a colorful garnish for these delightful appetizers. Line your serving tray with kale and garnish with the onions.

Shrimp and Tortellini Kabobs

Marinade

1½ **cups vegetable oil**

⅔ **cup red wine vinegar**

2 **teaspoons Dijon mustard**

2 **cloves garlic, minced**

1 **tablespoon dried Italian seasoning**

½ **teaspoon salt**

Kabobs

12 **ounces medium cooked shrimp (about 48)**

16 **ounces cheese-filled tortellini, cooked al dente**

48 **(4-inch) party picks**

Garnish

1 **cup fresh parsley or other greens, optional**

1 **tablespoon Parmesan cheese, freshly grated**

Combine marinade ingredients and mix well. Place shrimp in a ziplock bag or covered container. Place tortellini in a separate bag or container. Add 1 1/4 cups marinade to the tortellini and remaining marinade to the shrimp. Refrigerate for 8 to 24 hours, turning occasionally.

Remove shrimp and tortellini from the marinade and drain. Place one tortellini, one shrimp and then another tortellini on a party pick. Continue with remaining shrimp and tortellini. Arrange kabobs on a serving dish by placing in a circular pattern around a mound of parsley or other greens, if desired. Sprinkle lightly with Parmesan.

Makes 48

If you are in a hurry, substitute your favorite bottled Italian dressing (regular or non-fat) for the marinade.

Glazed Shrimp Kabobs

3 tablespoons vegetable oil

3 tablespoons apricot preserves

1 1/2 tablespoons white vinegar

2 1/4 teaspoons Dijon mustard

2 1/4 teaspoons curry powder

1 1/4 teaspoons garlic, minced

1 1/2 pounds large uncooked shrimp, peeled and deveined

12 (10-inch) bamboo skewers

Combine oil, preserves, vinegar, mustard, curry and garlic in a covered dish or ziplock bag. Add shrimp and refrigerate for 2 to 24 hours, turning occasionally.

Soak skewers in water for 20 minutes. Drain and thread shrimp on skewers. Grill or broil 6 inches from heat, turning until cooked through, about 3 minutes per side. Serve immediately.

Serves 6

This also makes a wonderful main dish!

Layered Tomato Pesto

1 ounce (about 12) non-oil-packed sun-dried tomatoes

3/4 cup boiling water

4 cloves garlic, minced

1/4 cup Parmesan cheese, grated

1/4 cup fresh parsley, chopped

1 tablespoon slivered almonds, toasted

1 teaspoon dried basil

1 teaspoon vegetable oil

2 (8-ounce) packages cream cheese, softened

Combine tomatoes and water in a bowl and let stand for 10 minutes or until tomatoes are softened. Drain well. Place tomatoes, garlic, Parmesan, parsley, almonds, basil and oil in a food processor and pulse until mixture is well minced.

Press half of the cream cheese into a 4-cup decorative mold which has been lined with plastic wrap. Spread tomato mixture on top of cream cheese. Spread remaining cream cheese on top of tomato mixture. Cover and chill for at least 3 hours.

Unmold and remove plastic wrap prior to serving. Serve with crackers.

Serves 18

Steamed Clams with Sherry and Herbs

3 tablespoons olive oil

3 tablespoons fresh garlic, crushed

2 tablespoons shallots, chopped

4 teaspoons fresh dill, chopped, or 1 teaspoon dried

4 teaspoons fresh parsley, chopped

1/2 teaspoon dried thyme

1/2 teaspoon black pepper

2 pounds fresh clams (about 4 dozen), rinsed and scrubbed

1 cup dry sherry

1 cup bottled clam juice

1/3 cup butter

1/4 cup green onions, sliced

sourdough bread

Heat olive oil in large, heavy saucepan over medium heat. Add garlic, shallots, herbs and pepper and sauté for 2 minutes. Add clams, sherry and clam juice. Cover and cook until clams open, about 5 minutes. Discard any clams that do not open. Add butter to the saucepan and stir until melted.

Transfer clams to a serving dish and ladle broth over clams. Garnish with green onions. Serve with warm sourdough bread.

Serves 8

This recipe doubles as an entree serving 4 people.

Phyllo-Wrapped Brie with Red Pepper Jelly

4   (12 x 16-inch) sheets
     phyllo dough, thawed

3   tablespoons butter, melted

1   (15-ounce) round brie cheese

2/3 cup red pepper jelly (recipe
     follows or use commercially-
     prepared)

Lightly brush one sheet of phyllo dough with melted butter. Place another sheet of phyllo on top of the first and brush again. Repeat with remaining sheets. Slice brie in half horizontally. Place one half on the center of the phyllo. Spread pepper jelly on brie and place remaining brie half on top. Wrap phyllo mixture up and over brie, pleating phyllo as needed to cover. Brush with remaining butter.

Place in a shallow baking dish. Bake at 400° for 15 minutes or until golden. Serve immediately with fruit or crackers.

Serves 8

Red Pepper Jelly

2   large red bell peppers (about 2
     cups), chopped

5   medium jalapeño peppers
     (about 1/2 cup), seeded and
     chopped

6 1/3 cups sugar

1 1/2 cups white vinegar

2   (3-ounce) pouches
     liquid pectin

Mix bell and jalapeño peppers with sugar and vinegar. Bring to a boil over high heat and continue boiling 1 minute. Reduce to medium-high and cook 4 minutes. Add pectin and boil one minute.

Pour jelly into sterilized jars and process in hot water bath for 10 minutes.

Makes 7 (1/2 pint) jars

This recipe makes a moderately-spiced jelly. To make it spicier, add more jalapeños. Pepper jelly can also be used on crackers with cream cheese, veggies in a pita, roast turkey sandwiches or grilled meats.

Walla Walla Sweet Squares

Crust

1/2 **cup butter, softened**

1/4 **cup sugar**

1 **cup yellow cornmeal**

2 **eggs**

1 **teaspoon salt**

1 1/2 **cups all-purpose flour**

Onion Topping

3 **tablespoons butter**

1 1/2 **tablespoons olive oil**

3 **pounds (about 12 cups) Walla Walla (or other) sweet onions, peeled and sliced 1/4-inch thick**

3 **teaspoons dried thyme**

1 **teaspoon salt**

1/2 **teaspoon black pepper**

3/4 **cup Swiss cheese, shredded**

Beat butter and sugar together. Add cornmeal, eggs and salt and beat until combined. Add flour and mix until combined. Press mixture into a 9 x 13-inch pan. Prick several times with a fork. Bake at 350° for 6 minutes. Remove from oven and cool.

Heat butter and olive oil in a large, heavy skillet over low heat. Add onions and sauté until onions are very tender, about 45 minutes. Season with thyme, salt and pepper. Stir in cheese.

Gently spread onion mixture over crust and bake at 325° for 30 minutes. Cool, cover and refrigerate for 8 to 24 hours. Before serving bring to room temperature or warm in a 200° oven for 20 minutes.

Cut into 2-inch squares.

Serves 8 to 10

Plan ahead by making these appetizers early. The flavors become more distinct the next day.

Frosted Spinach Torte

1 (8-ounce) package brick-style cream cheese, softened

1/2 cup cheddar cheese, shredded

1 (41/2-ounce) can diced green chilies

1/8 teaspoon garlic powder

1 (10-ounce) package frozen chopped spinach, thawed and drained

8 ounces ham, diced

8 (8-inch) flour tortillas

1 (8-ounce) tub soft-style cream cheese

2 tablespoons milk

1/4 cup fresh parsley, chopped

1/4 cup chives, chopped

Beat brick-style cream cheese, cheddar cheese, chilies and garlic powder with a mixer or processor until well combined. Divide mixture in half. Fold spinach into one part and ham into the other.

Place one tortilla on a serving plate. Evenly spread a generous 1/3 cup spinach mixture on top. Top with a second tortilla and evenly spread a generous 1/3 cup ham mixture on top. Repeat layers using five more tortillas, alternating mixtures. Spread final layer with spinach mixture.

Top with last tortilla. Beat soft-style cream cheese with enough milk to create desirable spreading consistency. Frost top and sides of torte with cream cheese. Garnish with parsley and fresh chives.

Chill until serving time. Cut into narrow wedges to serve.

Serves 24

For a change of pace, substitute crabmeat for the ham in this recipe.

Spinach and Feta Mushroom Caps

18 large fresh mushrooms

1 tablespoon olive oil

1 tablespoon butter

2 cloves garlic, minced

1/4 cup green onions,
    finely chopped

1 (10-ounce) package frozen
    chopped spinach, thawed
    and drained

2 tablespoons fresh parsley,
    chopped

1 teaspoon fresh thyme,
    chopped, or 1/4 teaspoon dried

1/2 teaspoon fresh rosemary,
    chopped, or pinch dried

1 tablespoon lemon juice

1/8 teaspoon salt

1/8 teaspoon black pepper

4 ounces feta cheese, crumbled

Gently twist stems from mushroom caps. Set caps aside and finely chop stems.

Heat oil and butter in a large skillet over medium heat. Sauté stems, garlic and onions until soft, about 8 minutes.

Add spinach and cook for 3 minutes. Add remaining ingredients and combine well. Remove from heat.

Stuff mushroom caps with spinach mixture and place on a baking sheet or pan. (Can be made ahead to this point and refrigerated for up to 6 hours.) Bake at 350° until mushrooms are thoroughly cooked, about 8 to 10 minutes. Serve warm.

Makes 18

Look for mushrooms that are firm and plump with tight, compact caps. When storing mushrooms, keep them loosely covered so air can circulate. This appetizer is also excellent as a side dish with grilled meats.

Mediterranean Skewers

Marinade

- 1/4 **cup lemon juice**
- 2 **tablespoons olive oil**
- 1 **tablespoon sugar**
- 1/4 **teaspoon salt**
- 1/4 **teaspoon dried tarragon**
- 1/4 **teaspoon black pepper**
- 2 **cloves garlic, crushed**

Skewers

- 3 **cups (8 ounces) whole fresh mushrooms**
- 2 **cups (2 small) zucchini, diagonally cut into 1/2-inch slices**
- 1/2 **cup red bell pepper, cut into 1/2-inch squares**
- **6-inch bamboo skewers**

Combine marinade ingredients and place in a covered dish or ziplock bag. Add mushrooms, zucchini and pepper. Refrigerate for 8 to 24 hours, turning occasionally.

To serve, thread vegetables on skewers and arrange on platter.

Serves 6

Bell peppers are actually a fruit and are available in green, red, yellow, purple and orange. Red bell peppers tend to be the sweetest, but don't hesitate to substitute one color for another.

Lamb and Melon Kabobs

Marinade

- **3 tablespoons olive oil**
- **2 tablespoons balsamic vinegar**
- **1½ teaspoons fresh rosemary, chopped, or ½ teaspoon dried, crumbled**
- **1 clove garlic, finely chopped**
- **½ teaspoon ground cumin**
- **½ teaspoon salt**
- **½ teaspoon black pepper**
- **¼ teaspoon cayenne pepper**
- **¼ teaspoon ground coriander**

Kabobs

- **1 pound lean lamb (leg or well-trimmed shoulder), cut into 1-inch cubes**
- **30 (1-inch) cubes cantaloupe**
- **30 (6-inch) bamboo skewers, soaked in water for 20 minutes**

Combine marinade ingredients and place in a covered dish or ziplock bag. Add lamb and refrigerate for 4 to 8 hours, turning occasionally.

Drain lamb and place on a broiler pan. Broil or grill, turning occasionally, until almost cooked through, about 4 minutes. Thread one piece of lamb and one cantaloupe cube on each skewer. Return to broiler or grill and cook, turning occasionally, until lamb is slightly charred on the outside, yet pink on inside, about 4 minutes.

Serves 12

When fresh herbs aren't available, you can substitute 1 teaspoon of crushed dried herbs for 1 tablespoon of snipped fresh herbs.

Korean Beef

2 tablespoons red wine

1/2 teaspoon black pepper

1/2 cup soy sauce

1/4 cup sugar

2 tablespoons green onions, chopped

1 teaspoon garlic, minced

2 tablespoons sesame oil

1 1/2 pounds sirloin steak, thinly sliced

12 (10-inch) bamboo skewers, soaked in water for 20 minutes

1/4 cup toasted sesame seeds

Combine wine, pepper, soy sauce, sugar, onions and garlic and let sit for 30 minutes to blend flavors. Pour sesame oil over steak and toss to coat. Add meat to marinade, cover and refrigerate for at least 2 hours.

When ready to cook, remove meat from marinade. Thread beef on skewers, leaving a few inches on one end. Grill or broil until meat is cooked to desired doneness. Sprinkle with sesame seeds and serve hot.

Makes 12 appetizer-sized servings

To slice the steak easily, partially freeze and then cut into thin slices.

Smoked Turkey in Endive

Filling

- 1/2 **cup fresh green beans, thinly sliced lengthwise**
- 4 **ounces smoked turkey breast cut into 1/4-inch cubes**
- 1/3 **cup red bell pepper, diced**
- 1/4 **cup shallots, minced**
- 2 **tablespoons fresh basil, minced, or 2 teaspoons dried**
- 2 **tablespoons Parmesan cheese, grated**
- 3 **tablespoons lemon juice**
- 1 **tablespoon olive oil**
- 2 **teaspoons capers, drained and minced**
- 1/2 **teaspoon freshly ground black pepper**

Endive Spears

- 25 **endive spears (about 3 heads)**
- 2 **tablespoons pine nuts, toasted**

Blanch beans in boiling water for 30 seconds. Drain and rinse in cold water until cool. Drain well and pat dry. Combine beans and remaining filling ingredients in a bowl. Cover and chill at least 1 hour.

Spoon mixture evenly into endive spears and sprinkle with pine nuts.

Serves 6 to 8

A tomato rosette is a perfect garnish. To add this special touch, slice a thin layer off the bottom of a tomato to form a base. With a paring knife, cut a continuous 1-inch spiral strip around the tomato. (Be careful not to break the strip.) Curl the peel tightly to resemble a rose.

Party Bread

2 packages yeast

1½ cups lukewarm water
(105°-115°)

1 tablespoon salt

1 teaspoon sugar

3 tablespoons vegetable oil

4 cups all-purpose or bread flour

1 egg

1 tablespoon water

12 ounces deli pepperoni,
thinly sliced

12 ounces provolone cheese,
sliced

Sprinkle yeast over the surface of the lukewarm water. Stir in salt and sugar and let stand for 5 minutes or until yeast has softened. Beat in oil and 3 cups of the flour by hand or with a heavy-duty mixer. Knead in the remaining flour. Continue kneading until dough is smooth, elastic and no longer sticky. Form dough into a ball and place in an oiled bowl. Turn dough over in bowl, cover with a light towel and let rise in a warm place until it has doubled in bulk, about 1 hour.

Punch down dough and turn out onto a lightly floured board. Divide into 2 portions. Roll one portion out to a 1/4-inch thick (about 7 x 14-inch) rectangle. Beat egg with water and brush dough with mixture.

Arrange half the pepperoni on dough, side by side, leaving approximately 1/2 inch on long edges. Arrange half the cheese on top of the pepperoni. Roll dough, jelly-roll fashion, and seal seam on bottom. Brush with egg mixture. Place on an ungreased cookie sheet and repeat process with remaining dough, pepperoni and cheese.

Bake at 375° until golden brown, about 20 to 25 minutes. Cool slightly on rack and slice into 1-inch slices. Can be made ahead, wrapped in foil and re-heated at 375° for 10 to 15 minutes.

Makes 2 loaves

This dough can be made in a snap using a bread machine on the dough cycle.

Roasted Red Pepper Crostini

24 (1/4-inch) French baguette
   slices (halved if large), toasted

 2 teaspoons olive oil

1/2 teaspoon garlic salt

3/4 cup roasted red peppers, sliced

1/4 cup Parmesan cheese

   freshly ground black pepper

Lightly brush toast slices with oil. Sprinkle with garlic salt. Place pepper slices on top of toasts. Sprinkle Parmesan over toasts. Grind pepper on top. Broil until cheese is just melted, 2 to 5 minutes.

Makes 24

To roast bell peppers, stem, seed and halve them. Lay peppers on a cookie sheet, skin side up, and broil until skins are well blackened, 5 to 8 minutes. Remove skins. Roasted peppers may also be purchased in the condiment area of many supermarkets.

Joanne's Spicy Shrimp Salsa

 2 large tomatoes or 1 (14-ounce)
   can whole tomatoes, drained

1/2 cup red onion, diced

1/8 cup (about 4) jalapeño
   peppers, seeded and diced

 8 ounces small bay shrimp

 1 tablespoon fresh cilantro,
   chopped, or 1 teaspoon dried

1/2 teaspoon cumin

 2 cloves garlic, minced

 4 teaspoons lime juice

1/2 teaspoon salt

1/4 teaspoon black pepper

Drop fresh tomatoes in a small pan of boiling water until skins blister, about 2 minutes. Remove from water, cool and remove skin. Coarsely chop fresh or canned tomatoes and place in a bowl. Stir in remaining ingredients. Cover and refrigerate at least 4 hours.

Serve with baked tortilla chips or as a side dish.

Makes 2 cups

For a thicker salsa, add all items except shrimp to the processor and pulse 3 times or until desired consistency. Stir in shrimp.

Black Bean Salsa

1 (16-ounce) can black beans, drained and rinsed

4 plum tomatoes, chopped

1/2 cup red onion, diced

1/2 cup green bell pepper, diced

1 (41/2-ounce) can chopped green chilies

1 clove garlic, minced

2 tablespoons fresh cilantro, chopped

3 tablespoons lime juice

1 tablespoon vegetable oil

11/2 teaspoons hot pepper sauce or to taste

1 teaspoon lime zest

1/2 teaspoon salt

Combine all ingredients in a medium-sized bowl. Cover and refrigerate for at least 8 hours. Serve with pita or baked tortilla chips.

Makes 3 cups

Look for fresh, undamaged bunches of cilantro with small stems. You can keep bunches of cilantro fresh in the refrigerator by clipping the stem ends and standing upright in 3 inches of cold water. Cover lightly with a plastic bag and chill for up to several days.

Dill Dip with a Twist

1 cup feta cheese, crumbled

1 cup sour cream

2 tablespoons lemon juice

2 tablespoons green onions, chopped

1 tablespoon parsley, chopped

2 cloves garlic, crushed

2 teaspoons fresh dill, chopped, or 1/2 teaspoon dried

1/4 teaspoon salt

1/8 teaspoon cayenne pepper

Combine all the ingredients in a bowl and chill for 1 to 24 hours. Serve with crunchy vegetables.

Makes 1 1/2 cups

The feta cheese gives this old stand-by a new twist!

Bleu Ribbon Dip

8 ounces bleu cheese, crumbled

2 cloves garlic, crushed

1/2 cup olive oil

2 tablespoons red wine vinegar

1 tablespoon lemon juice

1/2 cup red onion, chopped

1/2 cup fresh parsley, minced

1/4 teaspoon black pepper

Combine all the ingredients and spread into a shallow dish. Refrigerate for at least one hour or up to 2 days. Serve with baguette slices, crackers or fresh vegetables.

Makes 1 1/2 cups

A great do-ahead appetizer that is sure to take first place in the hearts of bleu cheese lovers!

Rave Reviews Dip

1 cup cheddar cheese, shredded

1 cup mayonnaise

1 (4½-ounce) can chopped green chilies

2 (2¼-ounce) cans sliced black olives, drained and divided

½ teaspoon hot pepper sauce

¾ cup green onions, chopped

¾ cup tomatoes, chopped

Combine cheese, mayonnaise, chilies, 1 can olives and hot pepper sauce. Spread into flat dish or pie plate and bake at 350° until hot and bubbly, about 20 minutes. Remove from oven and top with remaining olives, onions and tomatoes. Serve with tortilla chips.

Serves 6

Garden Herb Cheese Spread

1 (8-ounce) package feta cheese, crumbled

1 (8-ounce) package cream cheese, softened

1 tablespoon milk

3 large cloves garlic, crushed

1 tablespoon fresh parsley, chopped

½ teaspoon dried oregano

½ teaspoon dried thyme

¼ teaspoon black pepper

Place feta in a processor or blender and blend until creamy. Add cream cheese and milk and blend thoroughly. Add remaining ingredients and combine thoroughly. Chill for 1 to 24 hours. Serve with crackers or toast rounds.

Makes 2 cups

For a spectacular presentation, hollow out red cabbage or any color bell pepper and fill with spread.

Confetti Relish

1 (14-ounce) can white corn, drained

1 medium tomato, seeded and diced

1/2 cup green bell pepper, diced

1/2 cup red bell pepper, diced

10 black olives, drained and sliced

1/2 cup red onion, diced

3 green onions, chopped

1 jalapeño pepper, chopped

2 teaspoons olive oil

1 1/2 tablespoons cilantro, chopped

juice of 1 lime

1/8 teaspoon hot pepper sauce

1/4 teaspoon salt or to taste

1/8 teaspoon black pepper or to taste

Combine all ingredients and mix well. Cover and refrigerate until well chilled. Serve with reduced fat crackers or baked tortilla chips.

Makes 3 1/2 cups

To avoid getting the oils of hot chili peppers on your skin and in your eyes, wear rubber gloves or cover your hands with plastic sandwich bags while you are working with them.

Artichoke Relish with Pita Chips

Relish

- 1 **(14-ounce) can water-packed artichoke hearts, drained and chopped**
- 1 **(2-ounce) jar pimiento, drained**
- 2 **green onions, sliced**
- 3 **tablespoons Parmesan cheese, grated**
- 2 **cloves garlic, crushed**
- 2 **tablespoons lemon juice**
- 1 **tablespoon olive oil**
- 1/2 **teaspoon dried oregano**
- 1/8 **teaspoon black pepper**
- 1 **tablespoon fresh parsley, chopped**

Chips

- 4 **(8-inch) pita bread rounds**
  vegetable cooking spray

Combine relish ingredients in a bowl, cover and refrigerate for 8 to 24 hours.

Cut pita rounds into 8 wedges each. Pull each wedge apart into two pieces. Place wedges on a baking sheet that has been sprayed with cooking spray. Spray a light coating of cooking spray on top of wedges. Bake at 350° for 8 minutes or until lightly browned. Cool and store in an airtight container.

When ready to serve, place relish in a decorative bowl and surround with pita wedges.

Serves 16

These pita chips are a great alternative to taco or potato chips because they are low in fat. Sprinkle them with your favorite salt or seasoning before cooking and enjoy them without guilt!

Best-of-the-Best Artichoke Dip

1 (14-ounce) can artichoke
hearts, drained and
coarsely chopped

1/2 cup sour cream

1/2 cup mayonnaise

1/2 cup soft goat cheese, crumbled

1/4 cup Parmesan cheese, grated

1/4 cup green onions, chopped

1/4 teaspoon white pepper

Combine all ingredients and spread in a shallow baking dish. Bake at 350° until heated through, about 20 minutes. Serve with cocktail pumpernickel bread or crackers.

Serves 6

The addition of goat cheese gives this old favorite new life!

Fontina Quesadillas

2 teaspoons olive oil plus more
for frying, divided

1 cup frozen corn kernels,
thawed

2 jalapeño peppers, seeded
and minced

1/2 red bell pepper, diced

1 teaspoon dried oregano

8 (7-inch) flour tortillas

2 cups (about 8-ounces) Fontina
cheese, shredded

Heat 2 teaspoons oil in a large skillet over medium heat. Add corn, jalapeños, bell pepper and oregano. Sauté for 2 minutes. Remove from heat. (Can be made ahead to this point and refrigerated for up to 24 hours.)

Divide corn mixture and spread over 4 tortillas. Top each with 1/2 cup of cheese and another tortilla to create quesadillas. Brush skillet with oil and heat to medium. One at a time, cook quesadillas until they are brown and cheese melts, about 2 minutes per side. Cut each into 8 wedges and serve with your favorite salsa.

Serves 4 to 6

Feel free to substitute mozzarella cheese.

Blind Date Dip

4 large heads garlic, unpeeled

2¹/₂ tablespoons butter, thinly sliced

1 tablespoon olive oil

2¹/₂ cups chicken broth, divided

1 teaspoon dried basil

1 teaspoon dried oregano

1 teaspoon dried parsley

¹/₄ teaspoon black pepper or to taste

1 cup oil-packed sun-dried tomatoes, drained

5¹/₂ ounces goat cheese, sliced

¹/₂ cup fresh basil leaves for garnish

1 large french baguette, sliced

Slice 1/4 inch off tops of garlic heads (opposite root end) and remove any loose outer skin. Place garlic cut side up in an 8 x 8-inch baking dish. Arrange butter slices evenly over garlic. Drizzle oil over butter. Add 2 cups chicken broth to the dish and sprinkle with basil, oregano, parsley and pepper.

Bake at 375° until garlic is tender, about 1 hour and 15 minutes. Baste with broth every 15 minutes, adding additional broth if necessary.

Reduce heat to 325°. Transfer garlic to an oven-proof serving dish. Baste with 1/4 cup of the remaining broth from the baking dish. Arrange tomatoes and goat cheese around garlic and continue baking until cheese is almost melted, about 10 minutes. Garnish with basil and serve with bread.

Serves 6

... not much to look at, but it has great taste and personality!

Fabulous Fruit Dip

1/2 **cup dried apricots, chopped**

1 **cup orange juice**

1/2 **cup unsweetened applesauce**

1/2 **cup low-fat vanilla yogurt**

1/8 **teaspoon cinnamon**

dash ground ginger

Combine apricots and orange juice in a small non-aluminum sauce pan. Bring to a boil over medium heat. Cook at a reduced temperature, uncovered, for 15 minutes or until apricots are soft and liquid is absorbed, stirring frequently. Remove from heat, cover and let cool.

Place apricot mixture and remaining ingredients in a processor and process until smooth. Place in a bowl, cover and refrigerate at least 2 hours. Serve with assorted fresh fruit.

Makes 1 1/2 cups

Peppy Pecans

1 **cup sugar**

6 **tablespoons water**

2 **teaspoons salt**

1 **teaspoon cayenne pepper**

4 **cups pecan halves**

Combine sugar, water, salt and pepper in a large saucepan. Cook and stir over medium heat until sugar dissolves. Bring to a boil and cook for 2 minutes. Add pecans and stir until they are coated with mixture, about 1 minute.

Transfer pecans to a large buttered baking sheet. Spread evenly in a single layer. Bake at 350° until pecans are slightly brown, about 13 minutes. Transfer to wax paper, separating pecans if necessary. Cool completely. Store for up to 1 week in an airtight container.

Makes 4 cups

These are a perfect hostess gift for spice-lovers!

Apple Cider Surprise

1/3 cup lime juice

1/3 cup frozen lemonade concentrate, thawed

1 tablespoon grenadine syrup

1 (25 1/2-ounce) bottle sparkling apple cider

lime wedges for garnish, optional

Combine juice, concentrate and grenadine in a pitcher. Add cider and stir gently. Serve over ice and garnish with lime, if desired.

Serves 6 to 8

Cranberry Tea

3 cups boiling water

5 black-tea bags

1/2 cup brown sugar

3 cups cranberry juice cocktail

1/2 cup apple cider or white wine

cinnamon sticks, optional

Pour boiling water over tea bags, cover and allow to brew for 5 minutes. Remove tea bags. Combine tea, sugar, cranberry juice and cider in a large saucepan or crockpot.

Heat thoroughly, but do not boil. Add cinnamon sticks to individual cups, if desired.

Serves 6

This is also delicious served over ice!

Golden Cooler

2 cups sugar

3 cups boiling water

3 bananas, mashed

1/4 cup lemon juice

1 1/2 cups orange juice

1 (46-ounce) can pineapple juice

3 quarts ginger ale

Dissolve sugar in boiling water. Cool. Add bananas and juices. Combine well and freeze for several hours to 2 weeks. Remove from freezer 1 to 2 hours before serving and stir in ginger ale. Serving consistency should be slushy with frozen chunks.

Serves 20

Rum may be added to this deliciously different punch.

Conrad's Gin Fizz

1 (12-ounce) can frozen lemonade

4 3/4 cups milk

1 3/4 cups gin

2 eggs

3 tablespoons plus 1 teaspoon powdered sugar

1 tablespoon plus 1 teaspoon frozen orange juice concentrate

Blend all ingredients in a blender with 5 or 6 ice cubes. Serve immediately over ice.

Serves 8 to 10

You can vary the richness by using 1%, 2% or whole milk in this recipe.

Bull's Eye Bloody Mary

1 (32-ounce) can vegetable
cocktail juice

3 tablespoons steak sauce

2 teaspoons Worcestershire
sauce

1/2 teaspoon salt or to taste

1 teaspoon freshly ground black
pepper or to taste

juice of 1 lime

6 dashes hot pepper sauce
or to taste

vodka, optional

pickle spear, celery stalk or
pickled asparagus for garnish

In a pitcher combine all ingredients except vodka and garnish. Place ice in individual glasses and add 1 shot or desired amount of vodka. Top with juice mixture, stir, and garnish as desired.

Serves 8

These are wonderful with or without the vodka!

Iced Spiked Coffee

4 cups strong hot coffee

1/4 cup sugar

10 whole dried allspice berries

10 whole dried cloves

4 cinnamon sticks

1/2 cup coffee liqueur

1/4 cup half and half, optional

crushed ice

Combine coffee, sugar, allspice, cloves and cinnamon in a bowl. Cover bowl and let stand for 1 hour. Strain coffee and add liqueur and half and half, if desired. (May be made up to 24 hours ahead and refrigerated at this point.) Place crushed ice in a glass and add coffee mixture.

Serves 4

BREADS & BREAKFAST

Magnificent Apple Muffins
42

Lemon Muffins with Walnuts
43

Pecan Mini-Muffins
43

Banana Oatmeal Muffins
44

Cream Cheese Crescents
45

Cherry Scones
46

Golden Raisin Scones
47

Raspberry Kuchen
47

Huckleberry Streusel Coffee Cake
48

Apple Streusel Pizza
49

Raisin Oatmeal Bread
50

Quick & Healthy Wheat Bread
50

Dill Onion Bread
51

Golden Harvest Bread
52

Italian Breadsticks
53

Basic Bread Dough
54

Swiss Onion Bread Ring
55

Herb Rolls
56

Garlic Butter Buns
56

Picnic Pizza Bread
57

Cheese Filled Torta
58

Muffuletta
59

Bacon Topped Focaccia
60

Focaccia Bread with Brie
and Sun-Dried Tomatoes
61

Premiere Pizza
61

Baked French Toast
62

Swiss Cheese Breakfast Bake
63

No Guilt Strata
64

Pizza for Breakfast
65

Photo: Cherry Scones and No Guilt Strata   Sponsor: Great Harvest Bread Co.

Magnificent Apple Muffins

1 1/3 cups rolled oats

1 cup skim milk

1/3 cup brown sugar, packed

1/4 cup corn syrup

3 tablespoons vegetable oil

1 large egg white

3/4 cup all-purpose flour

1/2 cup whole wheat flour

1 1/2 teaspoons baking powder

1/2 teaspoon baking soda

1/2 teaspoon salt

1 teaspoon cinnamon

1/4 teaspoon nutmeg

1 1/4 cups (about 1 large) unpeeled Granny Smith apples, finely chopped

Combine oats, milk, sugar, corn syrup, oil and egg white in a medium bowl and let stand 5 minutes.

Combine flours, baking powder, baking soda, salt, cinnamon and nutmeg in a large bowl. Stir apples into flour mixture until evenly distributed. Stir milk mixture into flour mixture just until the dry ingredients are moistened.

Set rack in the upper third of oven and preheat to 425°. Spray muffin cups with cooking spray or line with paper baking cups. Divide batter among 12 muffin cups and bake 15 to 20 minutes, or until golden brown and springy to the touch. Let cool on a rack before serving.

Makes 12

Crisp, tart and juicy, Granny Smith apples are wonderful for both cooking and eating. When selecting apples, look for smooth, unbroken skins, without soft spots or bruises.

Lemon Muffins with Walnuts

1/2 cup unsalted butter, softened

1 cup plus 4 teaspoons sugar, divided

2 large eggs

1 teaspoon baking soda

2 teaspoons lemon peel, freshly grated

2 cups all-purpose flour

1 cup buttermilk

1/2 cup walnuts, chopped

1/4 cup lemon juice, freshly squeezed

Beat butter and 1 cup sugar with a mixer until creamy. Add eggs and beat well. Stir in baking soda and grated peel. Fold in 1 cup flour and then 1/2 cup buttermilk. Fold in remaining flour and buttermilk and then walnuts.

Pour 1/4 cup batter into muffin tins that have been buttered or lined with baking cups. Bake at 375° for 20 to 25 minutes until browned. Remove from oven and brush lemon juice over hot muffins. Sprinkle with remaining 4 teaspoons sugar.

Makes 12 to 16 muffins

For bite-sized muffins, reduce baking time to 12 to 15 minutes to make 36 mini-muffins.

Pecan Mini-Muffins

2 eggs, beaten

1 cup brown sugar, packed

1/3 cup butter, melted

1/2 cup all-purpose flour

1/4 teaspoon salt

1/2 teaspoon baking powder

1 teaspoon vanilla

3/4 cup pecans, finely chopped

Combine all ingredients and stir until well mixed. Grease two mini-muffin pans (or line with paper baking cups) and fill three-quarters full. Bake at 350° for 12 to 15 minutes. Remove from pan and allow to cool.

Makes 24

These muffins taste like a bite of pecan pie!

Banana Oatmeal Muffins

1 cup whole wheat flour

1 cup all-purpose flour

1 cup rolled oats

2 teaspoons baking powder

1 teaspoon baking soda

1/2 teaspoon cinnamon

1 egg

1 cup brown sugar

1/4 cup vegetable oil

1 cup plain non-fat yogurt

1/3 cup honey

1 teaspoon vanilla

1 cup ripe bananas (about 3 medium), mashed

vegetable cooking spray

Combine flours, oats, baking powder, baking soda and cinnamon and set aside. Combine egg, sugar, oil, yogurt, honey, vanilla and bananas. Add flour mixture and gently fold together until dry ingredients are moistened.

Spray muffin tins with cooking spray and fill three-quarters full. Bake at 375° for 20 to 25 minutes or until toothpick inserted in center comes out clean.

Makes 12 to 16 muffins

An ice cream scoop is handy for filling muffin tins.

Cream Cheese Crescents

Filling

   3 ounces cream cheese, softened

   3 tablespoons granulated sugar

   1/4 teaspoon almond extract

   1 teaspoon orange peel, grated

Dough

   1 (8-ounce) package refrigerator crescent roll dough

      vegetable cooking spray

Glaze

   1 cup powdered sugar

   2 tablespoons orange juice

   2 teaspoons orange peel, grated

   1 teaspoon butter, melted

   1/4 teaspoon almond extract

Blend filling ingredients with an electric mixer until smooth.

Open dough and separate into triangles following perforations. Spread filling over triangles, leaving 1/4-inch border on all sides. Roll up each crescent from bottom of triangle to top.

Place on a baking sheet that has been sprayed with cooking spray, forming crescent shapes.

Bake at 350° until light brown, about 15 minutes. Meanwhile, combine glaze ingredients and spread over hot crescents. Serve warm.

Serves 8

"Recycle" your orange and lemon rinds by grating them before discarding. Refrigerate grated rinds in a tightly covered container and use later to flavor breads and muffins.

Cherry Scones

3/4 cup dried sweet cherries

1 cup boiling water

3 cups all-purpose flour

3 tablespoons sugar

1 tablespoon baking powder

1/2 teaspoon salt

1/2 teaspoon cream of tartar

1/2 cup butter, softened

1 egg, separated

1/2 cup sour cream

3/4 cup half and half

1 1/2 teaspoons almond extract

additional sugar for topping

Soak cherries in boiling water for 10 minutes, drain and set aside.

Combine flour, sugar, baking powder, salt and cream of tartar in a large bowl. Cut in butter with a pastry blender or knife until mixture resembles coarse crumbs.

Combine egg yolk, sour cream, half and half and almond extract. Add to flour mixture and stir until soft dough forms.

Turn out dough onto a well-floured surface and knead gently 6 to 8 times. Knead in cherries until evenly distributed. Divide dough in half and shape into two balls. Pat each ball into a 6-inch circle. Cut each into 6 wedges with a sharp knife. Place scones on a lightly greased baking sheet.

Beat egg white until foamy. Brush top of scone with egg white and sprinkle generously with additional sugar.

Bake at 400° for 15 to 20 minutes.

Serves 12

Try these with dried cranberries too!

Golden Raisin Scones

2¹/₂ cups all-purpose flour

2¹/₂ teaspoons baking powder

3 tablespoons sugar, divided

1 teaspoon salt

¹/₄ cup butter, cut into small pieces

1 cup golden raisins

²/₃ cup plus 1 teaspoon milk, divided

2 eggs, lightly beaten

Combine flour, baking powder, 1 tablespoon sugar and salt. Cut in butter with a pastry blender or knife until mixture resembles coarse crumbs. Add raisins, 2/3 cup milk and eggs. Stir until evenly moistened.

Turn out dough onto a well-floured surface, knead gently until well combined and pat into a 9-inch circle. Cut into 8 wedges with a sharp knife. Place wedges on an ungreased cooking sheet and brush tops with remaining 1 teaspoon of milk. Sprinkle with remaining 2 tablespoons sugar. Bake at 450° for 15 to 18 minutes.

Serves 8

Raspberry Kuchen

1 egg, well beaten

1 cup sugar, divided

¹/₂ cup milk

2 tablespoons vegetable oil

1¹/₂ cups all-purpose flour, divided

2 teaspoons baking powder

1 cup fresh or frozen raspberries

3 tablespoons butter, chilled

Combine egg, 1/2 cup sugar, milk and oil in a bowl. Sift together 1 cup flour and baking powder. Stir into egg mixture and pour into a greased 8-inch square cake pan. Sprinkle raspberries over batter.

Combine remaining 1/2 cup flour and 1/2 cup sugar for topping in a small bowl. Cut in butter until mixture resembles coarse crumbs. Sprinkle topping over the raspberries. Bake at 375° for 25 to 30 minutes.

Serves 8

Huckleberry Streusel Coffee Cake

Streusel

   1/2 **cup all-purpose flour**

   1/4 **cup brown sugar, packed**

   1/2 **teaspoon cinnamon**

   1/4 **cup butter, softened**

   1/4 **cup pecans, chopped**

Batter

   1/3 **cup butter, softened**

   3/4 **cup sugar**

   1 **cup sour cream**

   2 **eggs**

   1/2 **teaspoon vanilla**

   2 **teaspoons baking powder**

   1/2 **teaspoon baking soda**

   1/4 **teaspoon salt**

  1 3/4 **cups all-purpose flour**

  1 1/2 **cups fresh or frozen
huckleberries or blueberries**

For the streusel, combine flour, brown sugar and cinnamon. Using a fork or pastry blender or knife, cut in butter until mixture resembles coarse crumbs. Stir in pecans and set aside.

For the batter, beat butter, sugar, sour cream, eggs and vanilla with an electric mixer at medium speed until well-blended. Add dry ingredients and beat until well-blended. Increase speed to high and beat for 5 minutes, scraping sides of bowl occasionally.

Pour batter into a 9-inch springform pan that has been sprayed with cooking spray or lightly buttered. Scatter huckleberries over batter. Sprinkle evenly with streusel mixture. Bake at 350° for 1 hour or until streusel is browned and toothpick comes out clean when inserted in center. Cool in pan on a wire rack. Remove sides from pan and serve.

Serves 12

Frozen berries will stay firmer if they are not thawed before adding them to the batter.

Apple Streusel Pizza

Cream Cheese Topping

   4 ounces cream cheese, softened

   2 tablespoons sugar

   1 tablespoon lemon juice

   1/4 teaspoon nutmeg

Apple Topping

   2 tablespoons butter

   2 large cooking apples, peeled and thinly sliced

   1/2 cup sugar

   2 tablespoons all-purpose flour

   1 teaspoon cinnamon

Streusel Topping

   1/3 cup sugar

   1/3 cup all-purpose flour

   1/4 cup butter, chilled

Pizza

   dough for a 12-inch pizza

   2 tablespoons sugar

   1 teaspoon cinnamon

For the cream cheese topping, blend all ingredients in a small bowl.

For the apple topping, melt butter in a large skillet over medium heat and add apple slices. Combine sugar, flour and cinnamon and stir into apples. Cook for 10 minutes, stirring occasionally.

For the streusel topping, combine all ingredients in a small bowl until crumbly.

Shape pizza dough into a 12-inch pizza pan or baking sheet, building up edges. Combine sugar and cinnamon and sprinkle over dough. Spread cream cheese topping over the cinnamon. Spoon apple topping over cream cheese and streusel topping over apple. Cover and let rise in a warm place for about 15 minutes. Bake at 375° for 25 to 30 minutes or until edges are golden brown. Serve warm.

Serves 8 to 10

Raisin Oatmeal Bread

2 cups quick-cooking rolled oats

2 cups all-purpose flour

1 teaspoon salt

1 teaspoon baking powder

1 teaspoon baking soda

1/3 cup sugar

1/2 cup light molasses

2 tablespoons vegetable oil

2 cups low-fat buttermilk

1 cup raisins

vegetable cooking spray

Combine oats, flour, salt, baking powder, baking soda and sugar in a medium bowl. Add molasses, oil and buttermilk and mix well. Fold in raisins. Pour into a loaf pan that has been sprayed with cooking spray and let rest at room temperature for 20 minutes.

Bake at 350° for 60 to 65 minutes. Remove from oven and cool on a rack for 20 minutes before removing bread from pan.

Serves 8

If you don't have buttermilk, you can substitute 2 cups of skim milk combined with 2 tablespoons of white vinegar.

Quick & Healthy Wheat Bread

1 cup all-purpose flour

2 cups whole wheat flour

1/3 cup brown sugar

1 1/2 teaspoons baking powder

1 teaspoon baking soda

1 teaspoon salt

1/3 cup wheat or oat bran

1/3 cup wheat germ

2 cups low-fat buttermilk

vegetable cooking spray

Mix all the ingredients except buttermilk and cooking spray in a bowl. Pour in buttermilk and stir until batter is evenly moist. Batter may be lumpy.

Spray a loaf pan with cooking spray and spread batter into it. Bake at 350° for 60 minutes. Remove from pan and cool slightly on a wire rack. Serve warm.

Serves 8

Dill Onion Bread

2 packages yeast

1/2 cup warm water

2 cups low-fat cottage cheese, room temperature

4 tablespoons butter, softened and divided

1/4 cup sugar

2 tablespoons onion, minced

4 teaspoons dried dill

2 teaspoons salt

1/2 teaspoon baking soda

2 eggs

5 cups all-purpose flour

vegetable cooking spray

salt to taste

Dissolve yeast in warm water and set aside.

Place cottage cheese, 2 tablespoons butter, sugar, onion, dill, salt, baking soda and eggs in a bowl and beat until combined. Add yeast mixture and beat until combined. Add flour, one cup at a time, beating well after each addition. Place in a greased bowl, cover and let rise in a warm place until doubled, about 1 hour.

Punch down dough and divide in half. Place dough in two 8-inch round casserole dishes that have been sprayed with cooking spray. Melt remaining 2 tablespoons butter and brush on top of dough. Sprinkle with desired amount of salt. Cover and let rise until doubled, about 30 minutes.

Bake at 350° for 40 minutes or until lightly browned.

Makes 2 loaves

This bread works best with a heavy duty mixer. You can also cut the ingredients in half and make the dough in your bread machine on the dough cycle.

Golden Harvest Bread

2 cups water

1/3 cup vegetable oil

1/4 cup honey

1/4 cup raisins

5 tablespoons brown sugar, divided

2 packages yeast

1/4 cup warm water

2 1/2 cups unbleached all-purpose flour, divided

3 cups whole wheat flour, divided

1 1/2 cups rye flour, divided

1/2 cup instant non-fat milk powder

2 1/2 teaspoons salt

2 tablespoons cornmeal

3 tablespoons butter, melted

Combine water, oil, honey, raisins and 4 tablespoons brown sugar in a blender or food processor and blend to liquefy. Dissolve yeast in warm water and stir in remaining 1 tablespoon brown sugar.

Combine 1 cup unbleached flour, 2 cups whole wheat flour, 1 cup rye flour, milk powder and salt in a large bowl. Add honey mixture and yeast mixture and beat with mixer on medium speed until smooth, about 2 minutes.

Combine remaining 1 1/2 cups unbleached flour, 1 cup whole wheat flour and 1/2 cup rye flour. Gradually stir in enough of remaining flours to make a soft dough that leaves the sides of the bowl. Turn out onto floured surface and knead until smooth and satiny, about 10 minutes.

Place dough in a lightly greased bowl, turning once to coat. Cover and let rise in a warm place until doubled in size, about 1 1/2 hours. Punch down dough and let stand for 10 minutes. Shape into 4 round loaves and place on 2 lightly greased baking sheets which have been sprinkled with corn meal. Cover and let rise again until doubled in size, about 1 hour.

Bake at 375° for 25 to 30 minutes. Remove from oven, brush with melted butter, and cool on wire racks.

Makes 4 loaves

Cover rising dough with plastic wrap or waxed paper coated with vegetable cooking spray to prevent sticking.

Italian Breadsticks

1 package yeast

2 tablespoons warm water

1 tablespoon sugar

4 cups unbleached white flour

1 1/2 teaspoons salt

1 1/4 cups cold water

1 tablespoon olive oil

vegetable cooking spray

1 egg white, well beaten

Toppings

sesame seeds, poppy seeds, garlic salt and/or coarse salt

Dissolve yeast in warm water. Stir in sugar and let stand for 5 minutes.

Place flour and salt in the bowl of a food processor. With machine running, add yeast mixture, cold water and oil. Process for 1 minute or until dough forms a ball, adding a little more water if dough is too dry. Process dough for 2 to 3 minutes in a processor or knead by hand for 4 to 5 minutes.

Place dough in a bowl that has been sprayed with cooking spray. Cover with plastic wrap. Let rise in a warm place until dough has almost doubled, about 1 hour.

Punch down dough and divide in half. Roll each half out into a 1/3-inch thick (about 10 x 14-inch) rectangle on a lightly floured surface. Cut each rectangle lengthwise into 1/2-inch wide strips. Arrange breadsticks one inch apart on a baking sheet that has been sprayed with cooking spray. Lightly brush the tops of the breadsticks with egg white and sprinkle with desired topping(s). Repeat with remaining dough.

Bake at 400° for 16 to 20 minutes or until golden brown. Remove from baking sheet and cool on a wire rack.

Makes 3 dozen

This dough can easily be made with a heavy-duty mixer which has a dough hook or by putting all the dough ingredients in a bread machine on the dough setting.

Basic Bread Dough

3 cups all-purpose flour

1 package yeast

1 tablespoon sugar

1/2 teaspoon salt

1 tablespoon butter

1 1/4 cups 2%, 1% or skim milk

Combine flour, yeast, sugar and salt in a large bowl or food processor until blended. Melt butter in a saucepan over medium heat. Add milk and heat until warm, about 130°.

To mix in a food processor, pour milk mixture into flour mixture while motor is running. Whirl until dough forms a ball and pulls away from sides of container, about 45 seconds. If dough clings to sides, add more flour, 1 tablespoon at a time.

To mix with a dough hook, pour milk mixture into flour mixture. Beat on low speed until evenly moistened, occasionally scraping flour to center of bowl. Beat on high until dough pulls away from sides, about 5 minutes. If dough clings to sides, add more flour, 1 tablespoon at a time.

To mix by hand, pour milk mixture into flour mixture and beat until dough is stretchy, about 6 minutes. Turn out dough onto a lightly floured board. Knead until smooth, about 10 minutes, adding flour as necessary to prevent sticking.

Turn out dough onto a lightly floured surface. Proceed as directed in Swiss Onion Bread Ring, Herb Rolls or Picnic Pizza Bread.

This dough can be made into a bread loaf by placing dough in a greased bowl. Turn dough over to grease top. Cover with plastic wrap and let rise in a warm place until doubled in size, about 45 minutes. Punch down dough and shape to fit into a loaf pan. Cover and let rise until doubled in size. Bake at 400° until brown, about 25 minutes.

Swiss Onion Bread Ring

1 recipe Basic Bread Dough, or
1 (1-pound) loaf frozen bread
dough, thawed

1/3 cup Swiss cheese, shredded

1 tablespoon butter, melted

1/4 cup onion, chopped

1 1/2 teaspoons poppy seeds

1/8 teaspoon salt

vegetable cooking spray or
vegetable oil

Cut dough into approximately 20 small pieces. Combine remaining ingredients except cooking spray in a small bowl and set aside.

Thoroughly spray or oil a bundt or tube pan. Dip top half of dough pieces in cheese mixture. Layer pieces in pan with cheese mixture on top. Spread remaining cheese mixture over and around dough in pan. Cover and let rise in a warm place until it has puffed up and almost doubled in size.

Bake at 375° for 25 to 30 minutes or until bread has evenly browned and is cooked through. Remove from pan by running a knife around edges and turning bread out onto a wire rack to cool. Break off pieces of bread to serve.

Serves 6 to 8

To create a warm, draft-free environment for dough to rise, turn your oven to its lowest setting for a few minutes. Switch the oven off and place your dough inside. If a microwave is more convenient, cook 1 cup of water long enough to boil for 45 seconds. Remove water from microwave, place dough inside and close the door.

Herb Rolls

1 recipe Basic Bread Dough, or 1 (1-pound) loaf frozen bread dough, thawed

1½ teaspoons thyme leaves, crushed

1½ teaspoons marjoram leaves, crushed

1½ teaspoons dried parsley

vegetable cooking spray

1 tablespoon butter, melted

Place dough in a bowl, cover and and let rise until doubled in size. Roll dough out on a lightly floured surface to an approximately 10 x 14-inch rectangle. Sprinkle dough with thyme, marjoram and parsley. Fold in half, pinch edges and roll out again to a similar size.

Cut dough into 12 pieces and shape into balls. Place balls in a muffin pan that has been sprayed with cooking spray, cover loosely and let rise in a warm place until doubled in size, about 30 minutes.

Bake at 400° for 12 to 15 minutes or until lightly browned. Remove from oven, brush with melted butter and cool on a rack.

Makes 12 rolls

Garlic Butter Buns

¼ cup unsalted butter, melted

1 tablespoon fresh parsley, finely chopped, or 1 teaspoon dried

1 tablespoon egg, beaten

1 teaspoon garlic salt

vegetable cooking spray

1 recipe Basic Bread Dough, or 1 (1-pound) bag frozen white or wheat bread rolls, thawed

Combine butter, parsley, egg and garlic salt. Spray a muffin tin or pie plate with cooking spray. If using Basic Bread Dough, shape into 12 rolls. Dip rolls into butter mixture and place in tin or pie plate. Spray plastic wrap with cooking spray, cover tin and let rise in a warm place until rolls have doubled in size, about 1 hour.

Bake at 350° until tops are golden brown, about 15 minutes for tins or 20 minutes for pie plate.

Makes 12 rolls

Picnic Pizza Bread

vegetable cooking spray

3 recipes Basic Bread Dough, or
3 (1-pound) loaves frozen
bread dough, thawed

1 1/2 cups cheddar cheese, shredded

1 3/4 cups mozzarella cheese,
shredded

3/4 cup Parmesan cheese, grated

3 tablespoons Italian herb
seasoning

Toppings, optional

1 (3 1/2-ounce) package
pepperoni

8 ounces sausage, cooked
and drained

1 (2 1/4-ounce) can sliced black
olives, drained

1/2 cup green onions, sliced

Spray two bundt pans with cooking spray. Cut each loaf of dough into 32 small pieces with a sharp knife. Place 24 pieces in each pan.

Combine cheeses and Italian seasoning. Measure 1 cup of cheese mixture and set aside. Sprinkle remaining cheese on top of dough in each pan.

Scatter toppings over cheese. Place remaining bread dough on top. Sprinkle with reserved cheese mixture.

Loosely cover bread and let rise in a warm place until it has doubled and is about 1 inch from the top of pan. Bake at 350° for 25 to 30 minutes. Cool slightly and invert onto a board. May be served hot, cold or at room temperature.

Serves 6 to 8

Customize this easy recipe to fit your own pizza preferences and take it along as a hearty no fuss addition to your next picnic!

Cheese Filled Torta

Dough

2 packages yeast

1 cup warm water

1/2 cup butter, softened

3 eggs

1 tablespoon sugar

1 teaspoon salt

4 cups all-purpose flour

1/2 cup Parmesan cheese, freshly grated

Bell Pepper Filling

1 tablespoon olive oil

1 cup onion, thinly sliced

1/2 cup red bell pepper, minced

1/2 cup green bell pepper, minced

1/2 teaspoon black pepper

3 cups Monterey Jack cheese, shredded

Artichoke Filling

1 (14-ounce) can artichoke hearts, drained and chopped

1/2 cup roasted red peppers, drained and chopped

1/4 cup green onions, chopped

2 cups Monterey Jack cheese, shredded

Glaze

1 egg beaten with 1 tablespoon milk

Sprinkle yeast over warm water in a large bowl. Stir until dissolved and let stand 5 minutes. Whisk in butter, eggs, sugar and salt. Add flour, 1 cup at a time, and mix until dough is smooth. Cover and refrigerate at least 2 hours. (Can be prepared up to 24 hours in advance.)

If preparing bell pepper filling, heat oil in a large skillet over low heat. Add onion and bell peppers and sauté for 15 minutes. Set aside to cool.

Divide dough in half. Roll one piece of dough into a 12-inch round on a lightly-floured surface. Place on a greased 12-inch pizza pan, pressing edges to form a 1/2-inch rim. Sprinkle dough with Parmesan.

Top with prepared bell pepper filling, black pepper and Monterey Jack, or, if using the artichoke filling, layer ingredients on top of Parmesan. Spread the filling to the edges of the crust.

Roll remaining dough out to a 12-inch round and cut into strips that are 1-inch wide. Weave strips in a lattice pattern over top, placing strips about 1-inch apart. Fold rim over strips, pinch to seal and flute. (Can be prepared up to 5 hours in advance. Cover and refrigerate. Return to room temperature before continuing.)

Let rise in warm place for 30 minutes. Brush dough with glaze and bake at 350° until brown, about 40 minutes.

Serves 10 to 12

Outstanding! Don't be intimidated - this is easier than it looks.

Muffuletta

1 (16-ounce) jar mixed pickled vegetables (giardiniera), drained and diced

1/2 cup pitted green olives, diced

1 tablespoon garlic, minced

1 teaspoon dried oregano

3 tablespoons olive oil

1 (1-pound) loaf focaccia bread, lightly browned

4 ounces dry salami, thinly sliced

4 ounces smoked ham, thinly sliced

4 ounces Fontina cheese, sliced

Combine vegetables, olives, garlic, oregano and olive oil. (Can be prepared up to 2 days ahead and refrigerated.)

Slice the bread in half horizontally. Arrange alternating layers of meat and cheese on bottom of loaf. Spread vegetable mixture over the top. Cover with top of focaccia. Wrap in foil and let stand for 2 hours at room temperature or up to 24 hours in the refrigerator.

Heat for 10 minutes at 350°, or until cheese melts. Cut into wedges to serve.

Serves 4 to 6

Skip the baking and serve this cold for an unusual picnic dish!

Bacon Topped Focaccia

1³/₄ **cups bread flour**

1 **package fast-rising yeast**

1 **teaspoon sugar**

³/₄ **teaspoon salt**

2 **tablespoons olive oil, divided**

³/₄ **cup hot water**

¹/₄ **cup black olives, chopped and drained**

4 **ounces (about 4 slices) lean bacon, chopped, with most of the fat trimmed and discarded**

1¹/₂ **cups onion, thinly sliced**

1¹/₂ **teaspoons fresh rosemary, chopped, or ¹/₂ teaspoon dried, crumbled**

¹/₂ **teaspoon freshly ground black pepper or to taste**

Combine flour, yeast, sugar and salt in a food processor. Pour 1 tablespoon plus 1 teaspoon oil into the water and then pour into processor while machine is running. Process until dough forms and then continue to process for 40 seconds. Add olives and process until combined.

Knead dough on a lightly floured surface until no longer sticky, adding flour if necessary. Spray a medium bowl with cooking spray or grease with olive oil, add dough and turn to coat surface. Cover with plastic wrap and let rise in a warm area until doubled in size, about 40 minutes.

Punch down dough and let rest 5 minutes. Spray or grease a baking sheet or pizza pan. Place dough on a lightly floured surface and roll to a 12-inch circle. Transfer to prepared pan, building edges up slightly. Let rise in a warm place for 15 minutes. Dimple surface of dough several times with the end of a wooden spoon or your fingertips. Build up edges again if necessary. Let rise an additional 15 minutes.

Heat 1 teaspoon oil in a medium skillet over medium heat. Add bacon, onion and rosemary and sauté for 5 minutes or until onion begins to soften. Remove from heat and set aside.

Brush dough with remaining 1 teaspoon oil and top with onion mixture. Sprinkle with pepper and bake at 375° for 30 to 40 minutes or until baked through. Cut into wedges for serving.

Serves 8

This also makes a wonderful appetizer!

Focaccia Bread with Brie and Sun-Dried Tomatoes

1 loaf focaccia bread

  olive oil

2 ounces brie cheese, sliced

1/4 cup (6 to 8) sun-dried tomatoes, rehydrated, or oil-packed, chopped

1/4 cup green onions, chopped

Brush focaccia lightly with oil. Layer brie, tomatoes and onions on top of focaccia. Bake at 350° for 10 to 15 minutes or until lightly browned and evenly warmed.

Serves 6 to 8

Focaccia is a flat Italian bread that can be made by hand or purchased in many supermarkets. Experiment to find your favorite toppings!

Premiere Pizza

1 12-inch pizza crust

1/2 cup goat cheese, crumbled

1 teaspoon dried thyme

10 to 12 whole fresh spinach leaves

1 (6-ounce) jar marinated artichoke hearts, drained and chopped

1 cup red onion, thinly sliced into rings

3 Roma tomatoes, sliced

1/4 cup Parmesan cheese, grated

Distribute goat cheese evenly over top of the pizza crust. Sprinkle with thyme. Place spinach leaves on top of cheese, using enough spinach to completely cover crust. Top with artichokes, onion rings, tomatoes and Parmesan.

Bake at 400° for 20 to 25 minutes or until pizza is cooked in the center.

Serves 6

Baked French Toast

vegetable cooking spray

1 pound loaf dense whole wheat bread, crusts trimmed and cut into 2-inch pieces

6 eggs

1½ cups half and half

1½ cups milk

¼ teaspoon nutmeg

¼ teaspoon cinnamon

1 teaspoon vanilla

½ cup butter, softened

1 cup brown sugar

¼ cup light corn syrup

1 cup pecans, chopped

Spray a 9 x 13-inch pan with cooking spray. Place bread in the pan. Combine eggs, half and half and milk. Pour over bread.

Blend nutmeg, cinnamon, vanilla, butter, brown sugar and corn syrup in a food processor until it becomes a paste-like consistency. Spread over bread and egg mixture. Sprinkle with pecans and bake at 350° for 30 to 45 minutes.

Serves 6 to 8

There is no need for syrup with this delectable breakfast dish!

Swiss Cheese Breakfast Bake

2 cups soft bread crumbs, without crusts

1 3/4 cups whole milk

8 eggs, lightly beaten

3/4 teaspoon salt

1/8 teaspoon black pepper

2 tablespoons butter

1/4 teaspoon seasoning salt

8 ounces Swiss cheese, sliced

2 tablespoons butter, melted

1/2 cup dry bread crumbs

8 slices bacon, cooked and crumbled

Combine soft bread crumbs and milk and soak for 5 minutes. Drain and reserve milk and bread. Combine reserved milk with eggs, salt and pepper.

Melt butter in a skillet over medium heat. Add egg mixture and scramble until soft but not fully cooked. Add soaked bread and pour into a 9-inch square or round baking dish.

Sprinkle with seasoning salt. Arrange cheese slices on top. Combine melted butter and dry bread crumbs and sprinkle over cheese. Top with bacon.

Bake at 400° for 10 to 15 minutes or until cheese bubbles on the edges and is melted in the center. Serve immediately.

Serves 8

No Guilt Strata

vegetable cooking spray

1 teaspoon vegetable oil

1 pound (about 4 medium) red potatoes, peeled, quartered and thinly sliced

5 large eggs

7 large egg whites

1 (16-ounce) container non-fat cottage cheese

1¼ cups (4 ounces) reduced-fat cheddar cheese, shredded

½ cup Parmesan cheese, grated

1½ cups (8 ounces) low-fat ham, diced

½ cup green onions, chopped

½ cup red bell pepper, chopped

⅓ cup all-purpose flour

1 teaspoon baking powder

½ teaspoon salt

½ teaspoon black pepper

Coat a large non-stick skillet with cooking spray, add oil and heat to medium-high. Add potatoes and sauté until tender and browned, about 14 minutes. Let cool slightly.

Whisk eggs and egg whites together in a large bowl. Add remaining ingredients and combine well.

Spray a 9 x 13-inch pan with cooking spray. Layer cooked potatoes in the bottom of the pan. Pour egg mixture over potatoes. Bake on a rack that is placed in the top third of the oven at 350° for 30 to 35 minutes or until golden on top and set in the center. Serve immediately.

Serves 12

Your guests will never guess this delicious strata is good for them!

Pizza for Breakfast

8 ounces bulk breakfast sausage

1 tablespoon butter

3 green onions, chopped

5 mushrooms, sliced

1/2 green pepper, diced

6 eggs

1 tablespoon milk

1/2 cup pizza sauce

1 Italian bread shell

1 cup mozzarella cheese, shredded

Cook sausage in a large skillet over medium heat. Drain well and set aside. Melt butter in a skillet and sauté onions, mushrooms and pepper until tender, about 5 minutes. Combine eggs and milk, add to skillet and scramble.

Spread pizza sauce on shell, top with egg and vegetable mixture, sausage and cheese. Bake at 350° for 8 to 10 minutes or until cheese is melted.

Serves 8

Don't save this pizza for breakfast - add a crisp salad and it makes a wonderful dinner.

SOUPS

Tuscan Soup
68

Tortellini Soup
69

Thea's Bean Soup
69

Italian Sausage and Bean Soup
70

Steptoe Butte Lentil Soup
71

Kielbasa Cabbage Soup
71

Tortilla Soup
72

Bay Scallop Chowder
73

Shrimp and St. Maries Wild Rice Soup
74

Mushroom Soup with Cashews
74

Thai Coconut Soup
75

Carrot Soup with Coriander
76

Cool Cucumber Soup
76

Greenbluff Apple Soup
77

Chilled Corn Soup
77

Photo: Steptoe Butte Lentil Soup, Cool Cucumber Soup and Carrot Soup with Coriander

Tuscan Soup

1 tablespoon olive oil

½ cup onion, diced

⅓ cup carrots, diced

½ cup red potatoes, diced

3 (14½-ounce) cans
chicken broth

¼ teaspoon dried marjoram

¼ teaspoon black pepper

1 cup water

1 (15-ounce) can cannelloni
(white kidney beans),
with liquid

⅔ cup tubetti macaroni or
orzo, uncooked

½ small head escarole (about 2
cups), thinly sliced

Heat oil in a large saucepan over medium heat. Add onion, carrots and potatoes. Sauté until lightly browned, about 5 minutes. Add chicken broth, marjoram, pepper and water. Bring to a boil, reduce heat, cover and simmer until vegetables are tender, about 10 minutes.

Add cannelloni and tubetti to saucepan and return to a boil. Reduce heat, cover and simmer until tubetti is tender, about 15 minutes, stirring occasionally.

Stir in escarole and heat thoroughly. Serve immediately.

Serves 4 to 6

Escarole, sometimes called broadleaf endive, has thick leaves and a slightly bitter flavor.

Tortellini Soup

1 tablespoon butter

4 cloves garlic, minced

2 (14½-ounce) cans chicken broth

6 fresh basil leaves, chopped, or 1 teaspoon dried

9 ounces fresh cheese-filled tortellini

½ bunch fresh spinach

1 (14-ounce) can stewed tomatoes

¼ cup Parmesan cheese, grated

Melt butter in a large saucepan over medium heat. Add garlic and sauté for 2 to 3 minutes. Add broth and basil and bring to a boil. Add tortellini and simmer, uncovered, until tortellini is tender, about 7 minutes.

Remove stems from spinach. Gradually add the spinach, tomatoes and cheese, stirring constantly. Heat thoroughly and serve immediately.

Serves 4 to 6

Thea's Bean Soup

16 ounces navy beans

3 (8-ounce) cans tomato sauce

5¾ cups water

1 cup celery, chopped

1 cup carrots, chopped

½ cup onion, chopped

4 cloves garlic, chopped

2 teaspoons salt

½ teaspoon crushed red pepper

½ teaspoon black pepper

Rinse beans in cold water. Cover with fresh water and soak for 8 hours. Drain well and combine all ingredients in a stock pot. Bring to a boil, cover, reduce heat and simmer for 2 hours, stirring occasionally.

Serves 6

When in a hurry, quick-soak beans by boiling them for 1 minute, covering the pot and letting them stand for 1 hour. Drain well and proceed with the recipe.

Italian Sausage and Bean Soup

1 **pound Italian bulk or link sausage, sweet or hot**

1 **tablespoon butter**

1 **cup onion, diced**

2 **cloves garlic, chopped**

1 **cup celery, diced**

1 **cup carrots, diced**

2 **cups potatoes, cut into 1/2-inch cubes**

6 **cups chicken broth**

1 **(15 1/2-ounce) can kidney beans, drained**

1 **(15 1/2-ounce) can Italian-style stewed tomatoes**

1/2 **teaspoon salt**

1/2 **teaspoon black pepper**

1/2 **teaspoon crushed red pepper**

1 **teaspoon chili powder**

Brown sausage in a deep skillet or saucepan over medium heat, remove and drain well. If using link sausage, cut into bite-sized pieces.

Melt butter in the same pan and sauté onion and garlic for 2 minutes. Add celery and carrots and sauté until onion is tender, about 2 minutes. Return sausage to pan and add remaining ingredients. Cover and simmer until potatoes are tender, about 1 hour.

Serves 6

To remove the fat from broth, gently lay a paper towel on the surface for a few minutes. Remove the paper towel and it will have soaked up a large portion of the fat!

Steptoe Butte Lentil Soup

1 pound dry lentils

3 (15½-ounce) cans beef broth

1 (14½-ounce) can zucchini
  with Italian-style tomato sauce

2 cups carrots, sliced

1 cup celery, sliced

2 cups onions, chopped

2 cloves garlic, minced

2 bay leaves

1 smoked ham hock

12 ounces smoked Polish
  Kielbasa sausage

Combine all ingredients except sausage in a stock pot. Add 5 3/4 cups water and bring to a boil. Reduce heat, cover and simmer until lentils are tender, about 2 hours.

Remove ham hock and bay leaves. Cut sausage into 1/2-inch chunks and add to soup. Heat thoroughly.

Makes 19 cups

The flavor of this hearty soup is even better the next day. It makes a big pot and leftovers freeze well!

Kielbasa Cabbage Soup

1 pound Polish Kielbasa sausage

3 cups cabbage, cored and
  coarsely chopped

2 (14½-ounce) cans
  chicken broth

3/4 cup onion, coarsely chopped

2 cloves garlic, chopped

1 (14½-ounce) can tomatoes
  with juice, chopped

2 teaspoons Hungarian paprika

1 (12-ounce) can beer

Cut sausage diagonally into 1/2-inch chunks. Place sausage and remaining ingredients into a stock pot and bring to a boil. Cover, reduce heat and simmer for 45 minutes.

Serves 6

You can make this soup in a snap by using pre-shredded coleslaw cabbage from the produce department in your grocery store. For a change of flavor add a few drops of hot pepper sauce.

Tortilla Soup

2 (16-ounce) cans tomatoes
with liquid

2 (8-ounce) cans tomato sauce

2 cloves garlic, minced

4 cups water

2 tablespoons sugar

1 tablespoon chili powder

1 teaspoon salt

1/2 teaspoon black pepper

1/2 teaspoon dried oregano

1 (41/2-ounce) can chopped
green chilies

1/2 cup tomato salsa

2 cups cooked chicken breast
meat, cubed

tortilla chips

Condiments

sour cream*

avocado*

shredded cheddar cheese*

chopped green onions

chopped black olives*

chopped tomatoes

Combine all ingredients except chips and condiments. Cover and simmer over low heat for 1 hour. When ready to serve, put a handful of chips in a bowl and add soup. Top with desired condiments.

Serves 8

Lite 'n Hearty certification applies only when the sour cream, avocado, cheese and olives are omitted.

Bay Scallop Chowder

1 tablespoon vegetable oil

1 cup onion, sliced

1 cup green bell pepper, thinly sliced

2 carrots, thinly sliced

1 tablespoon parsley, chopped

1 (28-ounce) can tomatoes with juice, chopped

1 (7 1/2-ounce) bottle clam juice

1/2 teaspoon salt

1 bay leaf

2 teaspoons steak sauce

3/4 teaspoon dried thyme

1 (14 1/2-ounce) can chicken broth

2 1/2 cups (about 2 medium) white potatoes, peeled and diced

1 pound bay scallops

Heat oil in a large saucepan over low heat. Sauté onion, pepper, carrots and parsley for 10 minutes. Add tomatoes, clam juice, salt, bay leaf, steak sauce, thyme and chicken broth, cover and simmer for 30 minutes. Add potatoes, cover and simmer until they are tender, about 25 minutes.

Remove bay leaf. Stir in scallops and cook until scallops are opaque, 2 to 3 minutes.

Serves 8

Shrimp and St. Maries Wild Rice Soup

1/4 **cup butter**

3 **slices bacon, chopped**

3/4 **cup carrots, diced**

3/4 **cup celery, diced**

3/4 **cup onion, diced**

4 **ounces wild rice, uncooked**

41/2 **cups chicken broth, divided**

1/4 **cup all-purpose flour**

2 **cups whipping cream**

11/2 **cups small shrimp**

Melt butter in a large stock pot over medium heat. Add bacon and vegetables and cook until vegetables are tender, about 5 minutes. Add rice and 3 1/2 cups of the broth. Cover and simmer 40 to 50 minutes or until rice is tender.

Stir flour into remaining 1 cup broth. Add to soup and stir until bubbly. Add cream and shrimp and heat thoroughly.

Serves 4

Mushroom Soup with Cashews

21/4 **tablespoons butter**

21/4 **tablespoons all-purpose flour**

12/3 **cups chicken broth**

1 **cup half and half**

1/8 **teaspoon ground nutmeg**

1/4 **teaspoon salt**

1/8 **teaspoon black pepper**

2 **cups mushrooms, sliced**

11/3 **cups cashews, coarsely chopped and divided**

whole cashews for garnish, optional

Melt butter in a large saucepan over medium heat. Stir in flour. Add broth, half and half, nutmeg, salt and pepper. Cook over medium heat, stirring constantly until mixture has thickened, about 10 minutes. Add mushrooms and half of the cashews and cook for an additional 2 minutes, stirring constantly.

Pour half of the soup mixture into a food processor or blender and process until fairly smooth. Repeat with remaining half of soup. (Can be made ahead and refrigerated up to 24 hours.)

Return soup to saucepan. Stir in remaining cashews and heat through. Garnish individual servings with whole cashews, if desired.

Serves 6

Thai Coconut Soup

4 **cups chicken broth**

2 **stalks lemon grass, cut into**
1/2-inch pieces

2 **teaspoons curry powder**

1 **cup boneless chicken meat,**
cut into small cubes

1/2 **cup straw mushrooms, halved**

4 **serrano chilies, sliced in**
half lengthwise, then cut into
half moons

3 **tablespoons fish sauce**
or soy sauce

1 **cup coconut milk, or 1 cup**
milk plus 1 tablespoon
coconut extract

2 **tablespoons lime juice**

2 **tablespoons fresh cilantro,**
chopped

3 **green onions, diced**

Bring chicken broth to a boil in a large saucepan. Add lemon grass and curry powder. Simmer uncovered for 10 minutes. Remove lemon grass from broth.

Add chicken and mushrooms, return to a boil and reduce heat. Stir in chilies and fish sauce, return to a boil and reduce heat again. Add coconut milk and return to a boil. Remove from heat and season with lime juice, cilantro and green onions. (If you multiply this recipe, be careful about adding additional chilies. Four is plenty, even if you triple the recipe.)

Serves 6

The results are worth the time it takes to find these interesting and unusual ingredients.

Carrot Soup with Coriander

1½ tablespoons butter

2 tablespoons shallots, minced

1½ teaspoons ground coriander

2 (14½-ounce) cans
chicken broth

1½ pounds carrots, peeled and
thinly sliced

½ cup whipping cream

1½ tablespoons fresh cilantro
leaves, chopped

½ teaspoon salt

¼ teaspoon black pepper

Melt butter in a heavy saucepan over medium heat. Sauté shallots and coriander for 2 minutes. Add broth and carrots and bring to a boil. Cover, reduce heat and simmer until vegetables are tender, about 35 minutes.

Pour half of the mixture into a blender or food processor and process until smooth. Repeat with remaining mixture. Return to saucepan and add cream, cilantro, salt and pepper. Heat through, but do not boil.

Serves 4 to 6

Cool Cucumber Soup

¼ cup olive oil

2 medium leeks, split lengthwise
and thinly sliced crosswise

3 garlic cloves, minced

1½ pounds cucumbers (about 2),
peeled, seeded and chopped

¾ teaspoon salt, divided

2 cups plain yogurt

2 cups chicken broth

¼ cup fresh basil leaves, chopped

¼ teaspoon black pepper

Heat the oil in a saucepan over medium heat. Add leeks and garlic and sauté until soft, about 4 minutes. Stir in the cucumbers and 1/4 teaspoon salt. Cook until the cucumber is just tender, about 12 minutes. Remove from heat.

Place cooked vegetable mixture in a blender, add yogurt and broth and purée until smooth. Chill until cold, about 1 hour. Stir in the basil, and season with remaining salt and pepper.

Serves 4 to 6

SOUPS

Greenbluff Apple Soup

4 small tart apples, pared
and quartered

1½ cups water

½ cup sugar cookie crumbs

2 tablespoons dry white wine

1 teaspoon lemon peel, grated

⅛ teaspoon cinnamon

1½ cups dry red wine

¼ cup sugar

4 teaspoons lemon juice

1 tablespoon seedless
raspberry preserves

Combine apples, water, crumbs, white wine, lemon peel and cinnamon in a large saucepan. Cover and cook over medium heat until apples are soft, about 20 minutes.

Strain and press apple mixture through a fine sieve, discarding solids. Return apple purée to saucepan. Add remaining ingredients. Heat over medium heat until sugar dissolves, about 2 minutes, stirring constantly. Refrigerate until well chilled, about 5 hours.

Serves 4

Chilled Corn Soup

6 ears sweet white corn, cooked
and corn removed from cob

1 cup chicken broth

2 tablespoons green onions,
white part only, chopped

½ teaspoon dried thyme

1 cup half and half

2 tablespoons fresh parsley,
minced

¼ teaspoon salt

¼ teaspoon black pepper

Place the corn, broth, onions and thyme in a processor or blender and blend until smooth. Strain mixture through a sieve, reserving all liquid and discarding all solids. Stir in half and half and parsley. Season with salt and pepper. Cover and chill for 1 hour or until cold.

Serves 4

Two (10-ounce) packages of frozen corn which have been thawed may be substituted for fresh corn.

SALADS

Asian Steak Salad
80

Spicy Steak and Pasta Salad
with Shiitake Mushrooms
81

Pacific Fresh Wild Rice Salad
82

Greek Orzo Salad with Shrimp
83

Incredible Couscous Salad
84

Tortellini with Peppers & Pine Nuts
85

Bulgar Salad with Lemon and Curry
86

Crispy Crouton Salad
87

Cashew Chicken Salad with Oranges
88

Chutney Chicken Salad
89

Mango Chutney
89

Lemon Mint Chicken Salad
90

Romaine, Gorgonzola and Walnut Salad
91

Sumptuous Raspberry Spinach Salad
91

New Potato & Asparagus Salad
92

Baby Pea Salad with Cashews
92

Favorite Fruit
93

Springtime Salad
93

Huckleberry Drizzle Salad
94

Jicama Orange Salad
95

Spinach Salad with Papaya Salsa
96

Arugula and Goat Cheese Salad
97

The Ultimate Endive Salad
98

Autumn Salad with Spicy Walnuts
99

Greens with Huckleberry Vinaigrette
100

Buttermilk Bleu Salad Dressing
100

Honey Mustard Dressing
101

Citrus Vinaigrette
101

Photo: Huckleberry Drizzle Salad

Sponsor: Sterling Savings Association

Asian Steak Salad

Dressing

- 1/4 **cup soy sauce**
- 3 **tablespoons rice vinegar**
- 2 1/2 **tablespoons peanut oil**
- 2 1/2 **tablespoons sesame oil**
- 1/2 **teaspoon fresh ginger, minced**
- 1/2 **teaspoon garlic, minced**
- 1/4 **teaspoon crushed red pepper**

Salad

- 2 **tablespoons butter**
- 1 1/2 **pounds flank steak, cut diagonally into 1/4-inch slices**
- 1/2 **teaspoon salt**
- 1/4 **teaspoon black pepper**
- 8 **cups mixed lettuce greens, rinsed and torn**
- 4 **cups fresh spinach leaves, rinsed and torn**
- 8 **ounces mushrooms, sliced**
- 2 **cups Walla Walla or other sweet onion, sliced into 1/4-inch rings**
- 4 **teaspoons sesame seeds, toasted**

Combine dressing ingredients and whisk until well-blended. (Can be made ahead and refrigerated. Bring to room temperature prior to serving.)

Melt butter in a large skillet over medium-high heat. Season steak with salt and pepper. Cook in batches for 45 seconds per side or to desired doneness.

Place lettuce, spinach and mushrooms in a large bowl and toss with desired amount of dressing. Top with warm steak, onion and sesame seeds. Serve immediately.

Serves 4

Substitute leftover steak that has been slightly warmed in the microwave to make this a super-quick summer salad.

Spicy Steak and Pasta Salad with Shiitake Mushrooms

8 green onions

1 tablespoon vegetable oil

8 ounces sirloin steak, trimmed and cut into 1/4-inch slices

8 ounces shiitake or cultivated mushrooms, washed, stemmed and cut into 1/4-inch slices

8 ounces spaghetti, cooked al dente

1 cucumber, peeled, seeded and cut into 1/4-inch slices

Dressing

3 tablespoons soy sauce

3 tablespoons balsamic vinegar

3 tablespoons rice wine vinegar

1/2 teaspoon crushed red pepper

2 teaspoons garlic, finely minced

1 teaspoon fresh ginger, finely minced

1/2 teaspoon sugar

1 tablespoon dark sesame oil

2 tablespoons sesame seeds, toasted

Chop the white part of the green onions. Slice top 3 inches of onions into thin rings and reserve.

Heat oil in a heavy skillet over medium heat. Add the beef and stir-fry for 30 seconds. Remove beef from the pan with a slotted spoon and place in a bowl. Add the mushrooms to the pan, reduce heat to medium and sauté for 5 minutes. Combine pasta, white part of green onions, beef, mushrooms and cucumber in a large bowl.

Combine dressing ingredients. Mix well and toss with the pasta mixture. Cover and chill for 1 to 24 hours, stirring occasionally. To serve, arrange the salad on individual plates and sprinkle with the reserved green onion rings.

Serves 6

Sesame seeds can be toasted in a dry frying pan over low heat until light brown. For a change, substitute boneless chicken breast or pork tenderloin for the beef.

Pacific Fresh Wild Rice Salad

Salad

  4 **cups chicken broth**

  1 **cup (6 ounces) wild rice, uncooked**

  2/3 **cup carrots, shredded**

  2/3 **cup red and/or green bell pepper, chopped**

  1 **cup zucchini, chopped**

  12 **ounces fresh crabmeat or imitation crabmeat, shredded**

Dressing

  2 **tablespoons white vinegar**

  1 **tablespoon olive oil**

  1/3 **cup onion, minced**

  3/4 **teaspoon dried oregano leaves, crumbled**

  1/2 **teaspoon dried basil, crumbled**

  1/2 **teaspoon sugar**

  1/4 **teaspoon salt**

  2 **teaspoons fresh or dried chives, snipped**

Bring chicken broth to a boil in a heavy saucepan and add rice. Cover and simmer over low heat until rice is very tender, about 60 minutes. Drain any remaining liquid from rice. Set aside to cool.

Combine carrots, peppers, zucchini and crabmeat in a large bowl. Combine dressing ingredients in a small bowl. Fold the rice into the crab mixture and toss with the dressing. Cover and chill for 1 to 12 hours prior to serving.

Serves 6

When using dried herbs, push them through a fine sieve with your fingertips to help release their flavor.

Greek Orzo Salad with Shrimp

Dressing

3 tablespoons fresh dill, chopped, or 1 tablespoon dried

1½ cloves garlic, minced

3 tablespoons olive oil

3 tablespoons lemon juice

1½ tablespoons red wine vinegar

½ teaspoon salt

¼ teaspoon freshly ground black pepper

Salad

1 pound large shrimp, cooked, peeled and chilled

¾ cup orzo, cooked according to package directions, rinsed, drained and chilled

3½ ounces feta cheese, crumbled

1 cup cherry tomatoes, cut in half

12 Kalamata olives

2 green onions, sliced

Combine dressing ingredients in a food processor or blender. Process until well-blended, about 15 seconds.

Combine salad ingredients and toss with desired amount of dressing. Serve immediately or refrigerate until ready to serve.

Serves 4 to 6

Garlic heads should be firm and compact, with no brown spots or sprouting. For the best flavor, peeled cloves should be bright white with no green core.

Incredible Couscous Salad

Salad

1 cup couscous, uncooked

1½ cups boiling water

¾ cup frozen corn, thawed

1¼ cups green and red bell peppers, chopped

1 (15-ounce) can black beans, drained and rinsed

¼ cup tomato, seeded and chopped

2 tablespoons green onions, sliced

2 tablespoons cilantro or parsley, chopped

4 cups smoked turkey breast, cut into ½-inch cubes

Dressing

⅓ cup olive oil

⅓ cup lime juice

¼ teaspoon salt or to taste

¼ teaspoon garlic powder

⅓ teaspoon cumin

pinch cayenne pepper

Garnish

Lettuce leaves

Fresh cilantro

Lime slices

Combine couscous and boiling water, cover and allow to stand 5 minutes. Uncover and cool completely.

Combine cooked couscous and remaining salad ingredients in a large bowl. Combine dressing ingredients in a small bowl and mix well. Pour over couscous and toss. Cover and refrigerate for at least 1 hour.

Line a serving platter with lettuce leaves. Spoon salad over lettuce and garnish with cilantro and lime slices.

Serves 4 to 6

This colorful salad is a favorite at lunch, yet hearty enough for dinner on a hot summer evening. Be sure to toss the couscous with 2 forks rather than a spoon. This will give the couscous more volume and prevent clumping.

Tortellini with Peppers & Pine Nuts

1/2 **cup balsamic vinegar**

1/4 **cup olive oil**

1 **teaspoon fresh basil, finely chopped, or 1/2 teaspoon dried**

1 **pound cheese-filled tortellini, cooked al dente**

3/4 **cup red bell pepper, cored, seeded and chopped**

3/4 **cup green bell pepper, cored, seeded and chopped**

1/2 **cup Romano cheese, grated**

1/2 **cup fresh parsley, chopped**

1/4 **teaspoon salt or to taste**

1/8 **teaspoon black pepper or to taste**

1/2 **cup green onions, sliced**

1/4 **cup pine nuts, toasted**

Combine vinegar, oil and basil. Toss with freshly cooked tortellini and cool to room temperature.

When cool, stir in peppers, cheese and parsley. Season with salt and pepper. (Salad may be made ahead and refrigerated.) Garnish with green onions and pine nuts and serve at room temperature.

Serves 4 to 6

To make this a main dish salad, toss in some crab or shrimp.

Bulgar Salad with Lemon and Curry

1 cup bulgar

2 cups boiling water

1 (15½-ounce) can garbanzo beans, rinsed and drained

2 celery stalks, thinly sliced

1 pound tomatoes (about 3 medium), seeded and diced

1 medium cucumber, seeded and cut into small chunks

½ cup fresh cilantro, minced

¼ teaspoon salt or to taste

Dressing

¼ cup lemon juice

1 teaspoon Dijon mustard

1 teaspoon curry powder

3 tablespoons vegetable oil

Combine bulgar and water in a large bowl. Cover and let stand until bulgar is soft and moist and most of the liquid is absorbed, about 1 hour.

Drain excess moisture from bulgar. Add beans, celery, tomatoes, cucumber and cilantro. Stir well.

Combine lemon juice, mustard and curry. Whisk in oil until dressing is well-blended. Pour over bulgar mixture. Stir well and season with salt.

Serves 8

Bulgar is a form of wheat with a unique nut-like flavor and texture which makes it delicious in salads.

*Substituted: parsley for cilantro
red pepper for tomatoes
added: 1 c. finely diced onion
1 lg clove garlic (or 3 small)*

Crispy Crouton Salad

Dressing

> 6 **tablespoons olive oil**
>
> 3 **tablespoons balsamic vinegar**
>
> 3 **cloves garlic, minced**
>
> 1/8 **teaspoon salt**
>
> 1/8 **teaspoon black pepper
> or to taste**

Salad

> 1 **pound tomatoes (about 2
> large), chopped**
>
> 1 **large yellow pepper, cut into
> 3/4-inch pieces**
>
> 6 **ounces mozzarella cheese, cut
> into 1/2-inch pieces**
>
> 1/3 **cup fresh basil,
> coarsely chopped**

Croutons

> 4 **ounces crusty Italian bread**

Garnish

> **fresh basil leaves for garnish,
> optional**

Whisk dressing ingredients together in a small bowl. Combine salad ingredients in a large bowl. Pour dressing over salad until evenly coated. Let stand at room temperature for up to 1 hour.

Cut bread into 3/4-inch cubes and toast under broiler, stirring occasionally, about 6 to 8 minutes until lightly browned. Just before serving, add croutons to salad and mix gently. Garnish with fresh basil leaves, if desired.

Serves 6

Cashew Chicken Salad with Oranges

Dressing

- 1/2 **cup frozen orange juice concentrate, thawed**
- 1/4 **cup parsley, chopped**
- 1/4 **cup vegetable oil**
- 1 **tablespoon red wine vinegar**
- 1 **tablespoon Dijon mustard**
- 1 **teaspoon grated orange rind**
- 1 **teaspoon sugar**
- 1 **teaspoon salt**
- 1/4 **teaspoon freshly ground black pepper or to taste**

Salad

- 6 **cups cooked chicken breast meat, cut into 1-inch cubes**
- 1/2 **cup celery, chopped**
- 2 **cups romaine lettuce, rinsed and torn**
- 1/4 **cup green onions, sliced**
- 1 **cup red bell pepper, cut into strips**
- 3/4 **cup salted cashews**
- 2 **oranges, peeled and sectioned**

Combine dressing ingredients in a processor or blender and mix for about 20 seconds. Set aside.

Gently toss chicken, celery, lettuce, onions, pepper and cashews with desired amount of dressing. Arrange oranges decoratively on top of salad. Serve immediately. (Can be prepared up to 8 hours ahead of time by omitting cashews and lettuce. Cover and refrigerate. Toss cashews and lettuce in just before serving.)

Serves 6 to 8

Chutney Chicken Salad

vegetable cooking spray

1 1/2 pounds boned chicken breast, skinned

2 tablespoons almonds, toasted and chopped

1 cup celery, sliced diagonally

1/2 cup green onions, sliced

3/4 cup mango chutney (recipe follows)

1 head romaine lettuce, cut into strips

Coat a large non-stick skillet with cooking spray. Add chicken and cook until done, about 7 minutes on each side. Remove chicken from skillet and slice thinly across the grain.

Combine chicken, almonds, celery, onions and chutney. Toss to coat. Spoon mixture onto individual plates which have been lined with lettuce. May be served hot or cold.

Serves 6

Mango Chutney

1 mango (about 1 pound)

2 cups Granny Smith apples

1/2 cup cider vinegar

1/4 cup sugar

1/4 cup brown sugar

1/4 cup red onion, chopped

1/4 cup black currants

3 cloves garlic, minced

1/2 teaspoon cinnamon

1/4 teaspoon allspice

1/8 teaspoon black pepper

1/8 teaspoon cayenne pepper

Peel and dice mango. Core, peel and dice apples. Combine mango, apples and remaining ingredients in a saucepan. Cook, uncovered, over medium heat for 20 to 25 minutes or until sauce thickens. Remove from heat, cool and refrigerate.

Makes 2 cups

This chutney is easy and versatile. Spread cream cheese on a plate and top with remaining chutney and sliced green onions. Serve with crackers for a spur-of-the-moment appetizer. It's also an exciting addition to a turkey sandwich.

Lemon Mint Chicken Salad

Salad

- **8 ounces bow tie pasta, cooked al dente**
- **3 cups cooked skinless chicken breast, cut into 1/2-inch cubes**
- **2 cups cantaloupe, cut into 1/2-inch cubes**
- **2 cups green or red grapes**
- **1/2 cup green onions, sliced**
- **11/2 cups celery, thinly sliced**

Dressing

- **1 (8-ounce) container low-fat lemon yogurt**
- **1/4 cup low-fat mayonnaise**
- **1 tablespoon fresh mint, chopped**
- **1 tablespoon lemon peel, grated**
- **3/4 teaspoon salt**
- **1/4 teaspoon black pepper**

Garnish

- **2 tablespoons slivered almonds, toasted**

Combine all salad ingredients in a large bowl and mix well. Combine all dressing ingredients in a medium bowl and mix well.

Toss salad with dressing. Cover and refrigerate for at least 3 hours to blend flavors. Just before serving, sprinkle with almonds.

Serves 12

One lemon yields about 2 teaspoons grated peel and 3 tablespoons juice.

Romaine, Gorgonzola and Walnut Salad

5 tablespoons extra virgin olive oil

1 tablespoon red wine vinegar

1/4 teaspoon salt

1/8 teaspoon black pepper

4 ounces Gorgonzola cheese, crumbled, brought to room temperature and divided

1/2 cup shelled walnuts, coarsely chopped and divided

1 head romaine lettuce, rinsed and torn

Whisk together oil, vinegar, salt and pepper. Mash half of the cheese and mix it into the oil and vinegar mixture. Stir in half of the walnuts. (May be made ahead to this point. Cover and refrigerate. Bring to room temperature before serving.)

Just before serving toss lettuce with dressing. Garnish with the rest of the cheese and nuts.

Serves 4 to 6

Sumptuous Raspberry Spinach Salad

Dressing

2 tablespoons raspberry vinegar

2 1/2 tablespoons raspberry jam

1/3 cup vegetable oil

Salad

8 cups spinach, rinsed and torn

1 cup walnuts, divided

1 cup fresh raspberries, divided

3 kiwis, peeled, sliced and divided

Mix vinegar and jam in a blender. Pour oil into the blender in a slow, steady stream and blend well.

Toss spinach, 1/2 cup walnuts, 1/2 cup raspberries and half of the kiwis with the dressing. Place spinach mixture in a large bowl and sprinkle with remaining walnuts, raspberries and kiwis. Serve immediately.

Serves 8

New Potato & Asparagus Salad

2 pounds (about 5 medium) new potatoes, halved lengthwise

1 pound asparagus, trimmed

1 tablespoon Dijon mustard

1 tablespoon lemon juice

1/4 cup olive oil

2 tablespoons chives, snipped

1/2 teaspoon salt

1/2 teaspoon black pepper

Add potatoes to a large pot of water, bring to a boil and cook until potatoes are tender, about 20 minutes. Drain, cool slightly and cut into wedges.

Add asparagus to a large pot of boiling water and cook until tender-crisp, about 8 minutes. Drain and rinse in cold water. Cut asparagus into 1 1/2-inch pieces. Toss potatoes and asparagus together in a large bowl.

Combine mustard and lemon juice in a small bowl. Gradually whisk in oil. Pour over salad. Add chives, salt and pepper and toss to coat. Serve at room temperature.

Serves 4

Baby Pea Salad with Cashews

1 (10-ounce) package frozen baby peas, thawed

4 slices bacon, cooked and crumbled, optional

1/2 cup celery, chopped

1/4 cup green onions, sliced

1/4 cup sour cream

1/4 cup mayonnaise

1/4 teaspoon salt

1 cup cashews, coarsely chopped

Combine all ingredients except cashews. Mix well and chill. Top with cashews just before serving.

Serves 6

Guaranteed to make a pea lover out of anyone!

Favorite Fruit

3/4 cup orange juice

1 (20-ounce) can unsweetened pineapple chunks, drained with juice reserved

2 tablespoons powdered sugar

8 to 9 cups fresh fruit, cut into bite-sized pieces (cantaloupe, grapes, muskmelon, watermelon, peaches, bananas, etc.)

Combine orange juice and the reserved pineapple juice. Whisk in powdered sugar until smooth.

Combine pineapple chunks and fresh fruit in a large bowl. If using bananas, do not add to bowl until just before serving. Pour juice mixture over fruit. Cover and refrigerate.

Serves 8 to 10

So simple and yet a big hit with kids. Use whatever fresh fruits are available.

Springtime Salad

Dressing

2/3 cup mayonnaise

1/2 cup sugar

2 tablespoons white vinegar

2 tablespoons milk

2 tablespoons poppy seeds

Salad

1 bunch romaine or other salad greens, rinsed and torn

1 cup strawberries, sliced

1/2 red or other sweet onion, sliced into rings

Combine dressing ingredients, cover and refrigerate for at least 2 hours.

Gently toss lettuce, strawberries and onion with desired amount of dressing just prior to serving.

Serves 4 to 6

Huckleberry Drizzle Salad

Dressing

- 1/4 **cup vegetable oil**
- 1 **tablespoon lemon juice**
- 1 **tablespoon white vinegar**
- 1 **clove garlic, minced**
- 1/4 **teaspoon salt**
- 1/4 **teaspoon sugar**
- 1/8 **teaspoon dry mustard**
- 1/8 **teaspoon onion salt**
- 1/8 **teaspoon paprika**
- 1/8 **teaspoon dried oregano**
- **pinch thyme**

Salad

- 8 **cups red and/or green leaf lettuce, rinsed and torn**
- 1/2 **cup blanched slivered almonds, toasted**
- 1/4 **cup feta cheese, crumbled**
- 1/2 **cup huckleberry syrup**

Combine dressing ingredients and blend well.

Toss lettuce with desired amount of dressing and place on individual salad plates. Sprinkle toasted almonds and feta cheese over each salad. Drizzle with desired amount of huckleberry syrup.

Serves 8

In a hurry? Substitute your favorite regular or low-fat bottled Italian dressing!

Toast almonds by baking at 350° in a single layer in a shallow baking pan for 8 to 12 minutes or until almonds are lightly browned, stirring occasionally.

Jicama Orange Salad

Dressing

- 1/3 **cup vegetable oil**
- 1/4 **cup white wine vinegar**
- 2 **tablespoons honey**
- 1 **tablespoon Dijon mustard**
- 1 1/2 **teaspoons caraway seeds, crushed**
- 1/2 **teaspoon orange peel, grated**
- 1/8 **teaspoon freshly ground black pepper**

Salad

- 2 **cups jicama, peeled and cut into julienne strips**
- 2 **cups red, green and/or orange bell peppers, cut into julienne strips**
- 8 **cups mixed greens, rinsed and torn**
- 2 **medium oranges, peeled and sliced crosswise**
- 4 **or 5 chives, snipped, optional**

Combine dressing ingredients and mix well. Place jicama and peppers in a bowl and toss with half the dressing. Cover and chill for 4 to 24 hours. Refrigerate remaining dressing.

Place greens in a large bowl. Drizzle desired amount of remaining dressing over the greens and toss. Arrange orange slices around the edge of the bowl. Add chives to jicama mixture, if desired, and spoon into the center of the salad. Serve immediately.

Serves 10

Jicama is a legume that grows underground. It is sweet, crisp and low in calories. If you've never tried it, you are missing a real treat!

Spinach Salad with Papaya Salsa

Salsa

- **1 cup canned black beans, rinsed and drained**
- **2 ripe papayas (about 1³/4 cups), peeled, seeded and diced**
- **1/2 cup red bell pepper, diced**
- **1/2 cup green bell pepper, diced**
- **3/4 cup pineapple juice**
- **1/2 cup freshly squeezed lime juice (about 4 limes)**
- **1/2 cup cilantro, chopped**
- **2 tablespoons cumin**
- **1/4 teaspoon salt or to taste**
- **1/8 teaspoon black pepper or to taste**
- **1/2 teaspoon crushed red pepper or to taste**

Salad

- **10 ounces fresh spinach, rinsed and torn**

Combine salsa ingredients and refrigerate for at least 4 hours. Toss spinach with desired amount of salsa and serve immediately.

Serves 6

Turn up the heat or tone it down by varying the amount of crushed red pepper. The salsa also makes a wonderful appetizer when served with chips or crackers.

Arugula and Goat Cheese Salad

8 ounces goat cheese

2 tablespoons parsley, chopped

1 tablespoon fresh tarragon, minced, or 1 teaspoon dried

1 tablespoon fresh oregano, minced, or 1 teaspoon dried

2 tablespoons green onions, chopped

1/2 teaspoon salt, divided

1/4 teaspoon black pepper, divided

1/2 cup olive oil, divided

1 cup dry bread crumbs

2 1/2 tablespoons balsamic or red wine vinegar

2 bunches arugula and additional mixed greens to total 8 cups, rinsed and torn

Cut goat cheese into 1/2-inch thick rounds and place in a baking dish. Combine parsley, tarragon, oregano, onions, 1/4 teaspoon salt and 1/8 teaspoon pepper. Sprinkle each side of the cheese slices with herb mixture. Drizzle 1/4 cup oil on top of the cheese and let stand at room temperature for 1 hour.

Remove cheese from oil and dredge in bread crumbs. Place on baking sheet and bake at 350° until soft, about 10 minutes.

Whisk vinegar and remaining 1/4 cup oil in a small bowl. Season with remaining 1/4 teaspoon salt and 1/8 teaspoon pepper. Toss with arugula, greens and warmed goat cheese and serve immediately.

Serves 8

Arugula, a member of the cabbage family, has a strong nutty flavor. It is well worth the effort to locate and try this unusual and delicious salad green!

The Ultimate Endive Salad

1 small (about 8 ounces) head curly endive, rinsed and dried

1 small head romaine, rinsed and dried

1/2 cup cilantro, chopped

1/3 cup green onions, sliced

1 cup broccoli florets

1/4 cup bleu cheese, crumbled

1/2 cup cranraisins, optional

2 large pears

2 1/2 tablespoons raspberry vinegar

1 tablespoon walnut oil

1/4 teaspoon salt or to taste

1/8 teaspoon black pepper or to taste

Stack endive leaves and thinly slice crosswise. Repeat with romaine. Combine endive, romaine, cilantro, onions, broccoli, bleu cheese and cranraisins in a large bowl.

Core and thinly slice pears and place on top of salad. Sprinkle with vinegar and oil. Toss gently and season with salt and pepper. Serve immediately.

Serves 6 to 8

Salad greens should be cold, crisp and dry. Rinse lettuce, spin dry and wrap in paper towels. Enclose lettuce and towels in a plastic bag and refrigerate for 1 to 48 hours. For added crispness, put greens in a metal bowl and place in the freezer for a few minutes before serving.

Autumn Salad with Spicy Walnuts

Walnuts

- 3 **tablespoons butter, melted**
- 1 **teaspoon salt**
- 1 **teaspoon cinnamon**
- 1/4 **teaspoon cayenne pepper**
  dash hot pepper sauce
- 1 1/4 **cups walnuts, coarsely chopped**

Dressing

- 3 **tablespoons red wine vinegar**
- 1/2 **cup olive oil**
- 1 **tablespoon plus 1 teaspoon Dijon mustard**

Salad

- 2 **heads red leaf lettuce, rinsed and torn**
- 1 **Granny Smith apple, cut into bite-sized chunks**
- 8 **ounces feta cheese, crumbled**

Combine butter, salt, cinnamon, pepper and hot pepper sauce. Add walnuts and stir to coat. Place nuts on a cookie sheet and bake at 300° for 15 minutes. Cool on foil.

Combine dressing ingredients and mix well.

Just before serving toss lettuce, apple, cheese and nuts with desired amount of dressing.

Serves 8 to 10

You might want to make extra walnuts because these spicy treats tend to disappear before the salad is tossed!

S A L A D S

Greens with Huckleberry Vinaigrette

Dressing

- 1/3 **cup huckleberry or raspberry vinegar**
- 1/2 **cup vegetable oil**
- 1 1/4 **teaspoons honey**
- 1/4 **teaspoon salt**
- 1/8 **teaspoon black pepper**

Salad

- 8 **cups mixed salad greens, rinsed and torn**

Place vinegar in a food processor or blender. Slowly add the oil while processing on high. Blend until mixture is slightly creamy. Add honey, salt and pepper and blend. Refrigerate.

Toss greens with desired amount of dressing just before serving.

Serves 8

For a hearty salad toss in some mandarin oranges, slices of avocado and sliced almonds. This vinaigrette is also excellent when served over melon and fresh fruit.

Buttermilk Bleu Salad Dressing

- 2 **cups regular or low-fat mayonnaise**
- 1/2 **cup regular or low-fat sour cream**
- 1/4 **cup low-fat buttermilk**
- 1 **teaspoon lemon juice**
- 1 **teaspoon white vinegar**
- 1/2 **teaspoon salt**
- 1/4 **teaspoon black pepper**
- 1/4 **teaspoon garlic powder**
- 4 **ounces bleu cheese, crumbled**

Combine all ingredients except bleu cheese and mix well. Gently stir in bleu cheese. Cover tightly and refrigerate overnight to blend flavors.

Makes 3 cups

SALADS

Honey Mustard Dressing

1 cup mayonnaise

2 tablespoons Dijon mustard

1/2 tablespoon dried
parsley flakes

1/3 teaspoon salt

1/2 teaspoon black pepper

1/2 tablespoon dried onion flakes

2 tablespoons vegetable oil

3 tablespoons red wine vinegar

3 tablespoons honey

Combine all ingredients except honey in a blender or food processor until well-blended. Add honey and continue to blend. Toss with your favorite salad greens.

Makes 2 cups

Keep a batch on hand in your refrigerator for a wonderful last-minute salad.

Citrus Vinaigrette

6 tablespoons balsamic vinegar

1/2 cup orange juice

1/4 cup lemon juice

1/4 cup olive oil

1/2 teaspoon dried marjoram

1/4 teaspoon salt

1/8 teaspoon black pepper

1/8 teaspoon cayenne pepper

Combine all ingredients and mix well. Cover and refrigerate for up to one week.

Makes 1 1/2 cups

PASTAS

Heavenly Marinara
104

Angel Hair Pasta with Crab and Pesto
105

Basil Pesto
105

Linguine with Garlic and Clam Sauce
106

Scallops Fettuccine
107

Browned Butter Sauce
107

Thai Chicken Fettuccine
108

Cajun Linguine
109

Basil Mushroom Fettuccine with Tomato
110

Baked Spinach Fettuccine
110

Cilantro Pesto Pasta
111

Tortellini Primavera
112

Popeye's Mostaccioli
113

Pasta Pancetta
113

Italian Sausage Pasta
114

The King of Italian Meat Sauces
115

President's Cannelloni
116

Mama B's Baked Ziti
117

Hearty Lasagna
118

Red Pepper and Gorgonzola Lasagna
119

Photo: Cajun Linguine and Italian Breadsticks

Heavenly Marinara

2 tablespoons olive oil

3 tablespoons onion,
  finely chopped

2 large cloves garlic, chopped

12 ounces bay scallops

3/4 cup dry white wine

1 (14-ounce) can Italian-style
  peeled tomatoes, drained
  and chopped

2 tablespoons fresh basil,
  chopped, or 2 teaspoons dried

1 tablespoon fresh parsley,
  chopped

3/4 teaspoon salt

1/4 teaspoon black pepper

16 ounces angel hair pasta,
  cooked al dente

Heat olive oil in a large skillet over medium heat. Add onion and garlic and sauté for 3 to 4 minutes. Add scallops and cook 2 to 3 minutes, turning once. Remove scallops from skillet and set aside. Add wine and bring to a boil over high heat. Cook until reduced by half, about 2 minutes.

Stir in tomatoes, basil, parsley, salt and pepper. Cook for 3 to 5 minutes until sauce thickens. Return scallops to the pan and cook 1 to 2 more minutes on medium heat until heated through. Place cooked pasta in a large bowl, toss with sauce and serve immediately.

Serves 4 to 6

For a change of pace, omit the pasta and serve the scallops with a loaf of crusty French bread to dip in the sauce.

Angel Hair Pasta with Crab and Pesto

2 tablespoons unsalted butter

1 cup fresh shiitake or
cultivated mushrooms,
washed, stemmed and sliced

1/2 cup basil pesto
(recipe follows)

1 large tomato, cored, seeded
and chopped

1 teaspoon lemon peel, grated

8 ounces fresh crabmeat, cooked

8 ounces angel hair pasta,
cooked al dente

Melt butter in a skillet over medium heat. Add mushrooms and sauté until tender, about 4 minutes. Stir in pesto, tomato and lemon peel. Add crab to sauce and heat through. Place pasta in a large bowl, toss with sauce and serve immediately.

Serves 4

If you are short on time, substitute a commercially-prepared pesto.

Basil Pesto

2 cups fresh basil leaves

4 cloves garlic, peeled

1/4 cup pine nuts

1/4 cup Parmesan cheese, grated

2 tablespoons lemon juice

2 tablespoons olive oil

Place basil, garlic, pine nuts, Parmesan and lemon juice in a food processor or blender. Slowly add olive oil while processing on high. Purée until well blended.

Makes 1 cup

Slightly lighter than many pesto recipes, this is sure to become an easy summer favorite. Make several batches when basil from your garden is bountiful - it freezes beautifully!

Linguine with Garlic and Clam Sauce

1 tablespoon butter

1/2 tablespoon olive oil

6 large cloves garlic, minced

3 (10-ounce) cans whole baby clams, drained and juice reserved

1/3 cup dry white wine

1 carrot, coarsely chopped

2 tablespoons fresh oregano, chopped, or 2 teaspoons dried

1/2 cup fresh parsley, minced and divided

1/8 teaspoon salt

1/4 teaspoon black pepper

12 ounces linguine, cooked al dente

1/2 cup Parmesan cheese, freshly grated

Heat butter and oil in a large skillet over low heat. Add garlic and cook until fragrant, about 1 minute. Add reserved clam juice, wine, carrot and oregano. Increase heat to high and boil until liquid is reduced to 1 1/3 cups, about 12 minutes.

Stir in clams and all but 1 tablespoon parsley. Simmer until just heated through, about 1 minute. Season with salt and pepper.

Add linguine to skillet and toss gently to blend. Transfer pasta to serving dish, garnish with reserved parsley and top with Parmesan.

Serves 4

Toss a dozen fresh clams in with the boiling pasta a few minutes before it is done. When the clams open their shells, remove from water, drain and set aside for a spectacular garnish!

Scallops Fettuccine

1/2 cup butter, divided

12 ounces scallops

1 cup red bell pepper (about 1 medium), chopped

1/8 teaspoon salt

1/4 teaspoon black pepper

1 cup sour cream

1 cup half and half

3/4 cup Parmesan cheese, grated

10 ounces fettuccine, cooked al dente

Melt 2 tablespoons butter in a skillet over medium heat. Add scallops and sauté until tender, about 2 minutes for small scallops. Add bell pepper, salt and pepper and remove from heat.

Melt remaining 6 tablespoons butter in a saucepan over low heat. Add sour cream and stir for 2 minutes. Add half and half and cook for 3 to 4 minutes, stirring constantly. Do not boil. Add Parmesan and stir until melted. Remove from heat and add scallops.

Place fettuccine in a pasta bowl and top with scallop sauce. Toss gently and serve immediately.

Serves 4

Browned Butter Sauce

1 cup butter

2 (15-ounce) cans tomato sauce

1 (14 1/2-ounce) can chicken broth

1 teaspoon fresh garlic, crushed

2 bay leaves

1 teaspoon dried oregano

1 teaspoon dried basil

Place butter in a deep pan and cook, uncovered, over medium heat until it is golden brown, about 8 minutes.

Combine remaining sauce ingredients in a large saucepan. Add browned butter and cook, uncovered, for one hour, stirring occasionally. Serve over pasta.

Serves 4 to 6

This sauce reduces to about 1 1/2 cups and is wonderful over your favorite cooked pasta.

Thai Chicken Fettuccine

Picanté sauce

- 1 (10½-ounce) can tomato purée
- 1 (4½-ounce) can chopped green chilies
- 2 tablespoons onion, minced
- 2 tablespoons green pepper, chopped
- 1 clove garlic, minced
- 1 teaspoon white vinegar
- ½ teaspoon salt
- ¼ teaspoon celery seed
- ¼ teaspoon crushed red pepper
- ⅛ teaspoon hot pepper sauce

Peanut sauce

- ¼ cup peanut butter
- 2 tablespoons honey
- 2 tablespoons orange juice
- 1 teaspoon soy sauce
- 1 teaspoon fresh ginger, grated

Fettuccine

- 8 ounces fettuccine, cooked al dente
- 3 boneless chicken breast halves, skinned
- 1 tablespoon vegetable oil
- ¼ cup fresh cilantro, chopped
- 2 tablespoons peanuts, chopped
- ¼ cup red bell pepper, thinly sliced

Combine picanté sauce ingredients in a medium saucepan. Bring to a boil, reduce heat and simmer, covered, for 10 minutes. Remove from heat and set aside.

Combine 1 cup of the picanté sauce and the peanut sauce ingredients in a medium saucepan. Cook over low heat until smooth. Remove from heat and set aside.

Toss cooked fettuccine with 1/4 cup of the picanté and peanut mixture. Place in serving bowl and set aside.

Cut chicken into 1-inch pieces. Heat oil in a large skillet and sauté chicken until brown and cooked through, about 4 to 6 minutes. Add remaining picanté and peanut mixture to chicken and stir well. Arrange chicken on top of fettuccine.

Sprinkle chicken with cilantro, peanuts and red pepper. Serve at room temperature with remaining picanté sauce on the side, if desired.

Serves 4

You can cut the preparation time by substituting 1 cup of commercial picanté sauce for the homemade sauce.

Cajun Linguine

1 (14½-ounce) can
chicken broth

1 (8-ounce) can tomato sauce

3 cloves garlic, minced

1½ teaspoons Cajun seasoning

½ teaspoon Italian seasoning

½ cup dry white wine

½ cup black olives, halved

¼ cup all-purpose flour

¼ teaspoon salt

⅛ teaspoon freshly ground
black pepper

4 boneless chicken breast halves,
skinned and cut into
½ x 3-inch strips

vegetable cooking spray

2 teaspoons olive oil

½ cup (about 2-ounces)
rehydrated sun-dried
tomatoes, julienne cut

1 pound linguine, cooked
al dente

Combine broth, tomato sauce, garlic, Cajun and Italian seasonings, wine and olives in a saucepan. Bring to a boil and simmer, uncovered, for 20 minutes.

Season flour with salt and pepper. Lightly dredge chicken in flour mixture. Spray a non-stick skillet with cooking spray, pour in olive oil and heat to medium. Add chicken and sauté until brown, 3 to 4 minutes. Stir in tomatoes and cook an additional 2 to 3 minutes. Pour in broth mixture and cook 5 minutes or until chicken is cooked through and sauce is slightly thickened.

Toss linguine with chicken and serve immediately.

Serves 4

Cajun seasoning can be found in the spice section of many supermarkets or you can make your own by combining the following: 1 tablespoon paprika; 2 1/2 teaspoons salt; 1 teaspoon garlic powder; 1 teaspoon onion powder; 1 teaspoon cayenne pepper; 3/4 teaspoon white pepper; 3/4 teaspoon black pepper; 1/2 teaspoon dried thyme; 1/2 teaspoon dried crushed oregano. Store leftovers in an airtight container.

Basil Mushroom Fettuccine with Tomato

1 **cup half and half**

1 **cup milk**

2 **tablespoons fresh basil, chopped, or 2 teaspoons dried**

3 **cloves garlic, finely chopped**

1 **cup mushrooms, sliced**

1/4 **teaspoon salt**

1 **pound fettuccine, cooked al dente**

1/2 **cup tomato, seeded and diced**

1/2 **cup Parmesan cheese, grated**

1/2 **teaspoon black pepper**

Heat half and half, milk, basil, garlic, mushrooms and salt in a large shallow saucepan over medium heat. Cook, uncovered, until sauce is reduced and thickened, about 20 minutes.

Toss fettuccine with sauce and tomato until well mixed. Top with Parmesan and pepper. Serve immediately.

Serves 4

Baked Spinach Fettuccine

1 **(10-ounce) package frozen chopped spinach**

2 **cups cottage cheese**

1/2 **cup Parmesan cheese, grated**

1/2 **cup sour cream**

3/4 **teaspoon salt**

1/4 **teaspoon dried thyme**

6 **ounces fettuccine, cooked al dente**

Thaw and drain spinach. Combine all ingredients except fettuccine and mix well. Stir in fettuccine and place in a covered casserole dish. Refrigerate until ready to bake or bake immediately at 350° for 45 minutes or until heated through.

Serves 6 to 8

Substituting non-fat ingredients won't change the rich flavor of this easy side dish!

Cilantro Pesto Pasta

Cilantro Pesto

1½ cups firmly packed fresh cilantro leaves

1½ cups firmly packed fresh flat leaf parsley leaves

2 tablespoons water

1½ tablespoons fresh lime juice

1 tablespoon olive oil

¼ teaspoon salt

3 cloves garlic, peeled

Pasta

vegetable cooking spray

2 tablespoons dry sherry

1 cup zucchini, sliced

1 cup green pepper, sliced

8 ounces angel hair pasta, cooked al dente

¼ cup rehydrated sun-dried tomatoes, chopped

½ cup Romano cheese, grated

3 tablespoons walnuts, chopped and lightly toasted

Place pesto ingredients in a blender or food processor bowl. Process until smooth, scraping sides occasionally.

Spray a heavy skillet with cooking spray. Add sherry, zucchini and green pepper. Sauté over medium-high heat for 5 to 7 minutes.

Place pasta in a serving bowl. Add pesto mixture, tomatoes, romano, walnuts and sautéed vegetables. Toss gently and serve immediately.

Serves 4 to 6

You can easily make your own "sun-dried" tomatoes. Cut Roma-style tomatoes in half and place skin-side down on a cookie sheet. Drizzle with olive oil and lightly salt each top. Bake at 200° for 8 hours. Cut into quarters and store in a jar of olive oil.

Tortellini Primavera

2 (10-ounce) packages meat or cheese tortellini

4 cups fresh vegetables such as colored bell peppers, zucchini, carrots and yellow squash, cut into chunks

3 tablespoons olive oil, divided

1/4 cup shallots, minced

3 cloves garlic, minced

1/2 cup oil-packed sun-dried tomatoes, coarsely chopped

1/3 cup fresh basil, chopped

1/2 cup fresh parsley, chopped

1 cup whipping cream

3 tablespoons dry white wine

1/2 teaspoon freshly ground black pepper

1/2 cup Parmesan cheese, freshly grated

Bring a large pot of water to a boil. Add tortellini and vegetables. Cook until tortellini are tender and vegetables are tender-crisp. Drain well, place in a large bowl and toss with 1 tablespoon oil.

Heat remaining 2 tablespoons oil in a large skillet over medium heat. Add shallots and garlic and sauté until softened, about 2 minutes. Stir in tomatoes, basil, parsley, cream, wine and pepper. Simmer, stirring occasionally, for 5 minutes. Pour sauce over pasta and vegetables and toss. Top with Parmesan. Serve immediately or keep warm in the oven and re-toss before serving.

Serves 4 to 6

We love this recipe because of its versatility. Besides being able to add whatever vegetables you have on hand - you can omit the cream (and calories) and still have a delicious meal!

Popeye's Mostaccioli

1 tablespoon butter

2 tablespoons olive oil, divided

1/3 cup pine nuts

5 cloves garlic, minced

2 (10-ounce) packages frozen chopped spinach

1 (14 1/2-ounce) can chopped tomatoes, drained

1 pound mostaccioli or penne pasta, cooked al dente

12 ounces feta cheese, crumbled

1/2 teaspoon salt

1/4 teaspoon black pepper

Melt butter and 1 tablespoon oil in a large skillet over medium heat. Add pine nuts and garlic and sauté until pine nuts are light brown, about 5 minutes. Thaw and drain spinach. Add spinach and tomatoes and sauté until heated through, about 3 minutes.

Place cooked pasta in a large bowl and toss with remaining 1 tablespoon oil. Top with spinach mixture, feta, salt and pepper and toss well. Serve immediately.

Serves 6

Mostaccioli - "little mustaches" - are similar in shape to penne, but shorter.

Pasta Pancetta

1/4 pound pancetta or smoked bacon, diced

1/2 teaspoon crushed red pepper

1/2 cup dry white wine

1 (14 1/2-ounce) can stewed tomatoes

6 ounces mostaccioli pasta, cooked al dente

1/2 cup Parmesan cheese, grated

Cook pancetta in a skillet over medium heat until cooked, but not crisp. Drain all but 2 teaspoons grease from pan. Add red pepper and sauté for 1 minute. Add wine and stewed tomatoes and cook over medium heat until slightly thickened, about 12 minutes.

Combine pasta and sauce and top with Parmesan.

Serves 2

Pancetta is an Italian bacon that can be found in Italian markets or delicatessens.

Italian Sausage Pasta

Sauce

   vegetable cooking spray

1   cup onion, chopped

3   cloves garlic, minced

1   (14-ounce) can whole
   tomatoes with juice, chopped

1   (8-ounce) can tomato sauce

1   (6-ounce) can tomato paste

1/4   cup fresh parsley, chopped

1   tablespoon red wine vinegar

1   teaspoon dried oregano

1   teaspoon dried basil

1   bay leaf

1/2   teaspoon salt

1/2   teaspoon crushed red pepper

1   pound smoked Italian sausage
   links, cut diagonally into
   1-inch chunks and then
   quartered

Pasta

8   ounces penne or other pasta,
   cooked al dente

Coat a saucepan with cooking spray and heat to medium. Add onion and garlic and sauté until soft, about 5 minutes. Add remaining sauce ingredients, except sausage, cover and simmer for 25 minutes. Add sausage and cook for an additional 5 minutes. Serve sauce on top of hot pasta.

Serves 4

Ounce for ounce, dried, crushed chili peppers pack more punch than fresh. Drying intensifies and magnifies the flavors.

The King of Italian Meat Sauces

Sauce

1½ **cups onion, chopped**

1 **pound extra-lean ground beef and/or bulk Italian sausage**

4 **cloves garlic, minced**

3 **(14½-ounce) cans Italian-style stewed tomatoes with oregano and basil**

1 **(6-ounce) can tomato paste**

¼ **cup parsley, chopped**

¼ **cup brown sugar**

1 **teaspoon salt**

⅛ **teaspoon black pepper**

1½ **teaspoons dried oregano, crushed**

¼ **teaspoon dried thyme**

2 **bay leaves**

⅛ **teaspoon cayenne pepper**

2 **cups water**

Pasta

2 **pounds linguine, cooked al dente**

¼ **cup Parmesan cheese, freshly grated, optional**

Combine onion, meat and garlic in a Dutch oven and cook until meat is brown and onion is tender. Drain off any fat. Add remaining sauce ingredients. Simmer, uncovered, until sauce has thickened, about 2 hours, stirring occasionally.

Remove bay leaves. Serve over hot linguine and top with Parmesan, if desired.

Serves 6 to 8

Small amounts of salt and oil added to water when cooking pasta will shorten cooking time and reduce sticking.

President's Cannelloni

Pasta

  2 **cups all-purpose flour**

  1 **tablespoon salt**

  2 **eggs, lightly beaten**

      up to 5 tablespoons water

Red Sauce

  2 **tablespoons olive oil**

  1/3 **cup onion, chopped**

  1/4 **cup fresh parsley, minced**

  3 **cloves garlic, minced**

  2 **(14 1/2-ounce) cans whole tomatoes with juice, chopped**

  1 **(6-ounce) can tomato paste**

White Sauce

  1/4 **cup butter**

  1/4 **cup all-purpose flour**

  2 **cups milk**

  1 **teaspoon salt**

  1/8 **teaspoon nutmeg**

  1/4 **cup Parmesan cheese, grated**

Filling

  1 **(16-ounce) container ricotta cheese**

  1/2 **cup Parmesan cheese, grated**

  1 **(10-ounce) package frozen chopped spinach, thawed and well drained**

Topping

  1/2 **cup Parmesan cheese, grated**

For the pasta, combine flour and salt. Stir eggs into flour and add water 1 tablespoon at a time until a stiff dough is formed. Turn out dough onto a floured surface and knead until smooth, about 5 minutes. Divide dough in half and roll out each half until paper thin. Cut into 4-inch squares. Drop squares two at a time into boiling water for 15 seconds. Remove and plunge into cold water for 15 seconds. Drain on cloth towels. Cover until ready to use.

For the red sauce, heat oil in a skillet over medium heat. Add onion, parsley and garlic and sauté until onion is soft, about 5 minutes. Add tomatoes and tomato paste and simmer, uncovered, for 15 minutes.

For the white sauce, melt butter in a saucepan. Add flour and stir to make a paste. Slowly add milk, stirring constantly. Add salt, nutmeg and Parmesan. Stir until sauce thickens, about 10 minutes.

For the filling, combine ricotta, Parmesan and spinach.

To assemble, spoon one cup of red sauce on bottom of a 9 x 13-inch baking dish. Spread a small amount of filling toward the edge of each pasta square. Roll and place seam side down on top of sauce. Spread white sauce on top of cannelloni. Top with remaining red sauce and Parmesan. Cover with foil. Bake at 350° for 1 hour, removing foil half way through baking time. Serve with additional Parmesan, if desired.

Serves 6 to 8

Mama B's Baked Ziti

Sauce

- 3 tablespoons olive oil
- 1 cup onion, finely chopped
- 4 large cloves garlic, minced
- 2 (28-ounce) cans plum tomatoes, puréed in blender
- 1 (6-ounce) can tomato paste
- 1½ tablespoons fresh basil, minced, or 2 teaspoons dried
- 1 tablespoon fresh oregano, minced, or 1 teaspoon dried
- 1 teaspoon salt
- ¼ teaspoon black pepper

Filling

- 1 (16-ounce) container ricotta cheese
- ¼ cup plus 3 tablespoons Parmesan cheese, divided
- 3 cups mozzarella cheese, shredded and divided
- ½ teaspoon salt
- ¼ teaspoon black pepper

Pasta

- 1 (16-ounce) package ziti or rigatoni pasta, cooked al dente

For the sauce, heat oil in a large saucepan. Add onion and sauté for 2 minutes. Add garlic and sauté until onion is translucent, about 4 minutes. Add remaining sauce ingredients and simmer gently, uncovered, for 1 hour.

Combine ricotta, 1/4 cup Parmesan, 1 cup mozzarella, salt and pepper. Add pasta and 1 cup tomato sauce to the cheese mixture and combine well. Spread mixture in the bottom of a 9 x 13-inch baking dish. Pour 3 cups tomato sauce on top. Sprinkle with remaining 2 cups mozzarella and 3 tablespoons Parmesan. (Can be prepared up to 24 hours in advance and refrigerated until ready to bake.) Cover with foil and bake at 350° for 25 minutes. Remove foil and bake until hot and bubbly, about 10 minutes. Serve with remaining sauce, if desired.

Serves 8

Substitute 3 cups of your favorite bottled tomato sauce to make this meatless main dish in a hurry. Pepperoni or ground beef can be added if your family prefers.

Hearty Lasagna

vegetable cooking spray
1/2 **pound extra-lean ground beef**
1 **cup onion, chopped**
3 **cloves garlic, minced**
Sauce
1 **(14-ounce) can whole**
tomatoes with juice, chopped
1 **(8-ounce) can tomato sauce**
1 **(6-ounce) can tomato paste**
1/4 **cup fresh parsley, chopped**
1 **tablespoon red wine vinegar**
1 **teaspoon dried oregano**
1 **teaspoon dried basil**
1 **bay leaf**
1/2 **teaspoon salt**
1/2 **teaspoon crushed red pepper**
Filling
1 **(16-ounce) container non-fat**
cottage cheese
2 **tablespoons freshly grated**
Parmesan cheese
1 **egg white**
2 **tablespoons fresh parsley**
1 **teaspoon dried basil**
Pasta
8 **lasagna noodles, uncooked**
1 1/2 **cups (6-ounces) reduced-fat**
mozzarella cheese, shredded
and divided
2 **tablespoons Parmesan cheese**

Coat a large saucepan with cooking spray, add ground beef, onion and garlic. Cook and stir until meat is browned and crumbled and onion is tender, about 5 minutes. Drain meat on paper towels and wipe drippings from pan.

Return meat mixture to pan, add sauce ingredients and bring to a boil. Cover, reduce heat and simmer for 30 minutes, stirring occasionally. Remove bay leaf and set meat sauce aside.

Combine filling ingredients in a medium bowl and set aside.

Place 1 1/3 cups meat sauce in the bottom of an 8 x 12-inch or a 10 x 10-inch pan. Top with 4 uncooked noodles. Spread half the filling mixture on top of noodles. Top with 3/4 cup mozzarella.

Repeat layer with meat sauce, noodles and filling mixture. Top with remaining meat sauce. (May be made ahead, covered and refrigerated at this point.)

Cover with foil and bake at 375° for about 1 hour (1 hour and 30 minutes if refrigerated before baking). Remove foil and sprinkle with remaining mozzarella and 2 tablespoons Parmesan. Replace foil and let stand for about 10 minutes before serving.

Serves 8

This lasagna is a snap to prepare because you don't have to pre-cook the noodles. It will quickly become a family favorite - easy, healthy, hearty and delicious!

Red Pepper and Gorgonzola Lasagna

4 **red bell peppers**

2 **red onions, cut into**
1/2-inch slices

3/4 **teaspoon dried thyme, divided**

2 **tablespoons olive oil**

1 **head escarole, rinsed,**
trimmed and sliced crosswise
into 1-inch strips

1/4 **teaspoon salt**

1/4 **teaspoon freshly ground**
black pepper

9 **lasagna noodles, cooked**
al dente

1/4 **cup Parmesan cheese, freshly**
grated and divided

4 **ounces Gorgonzola cheese,**
crumbled

Place peppers in the center of a baking sheet and surround with onion slices. Broil for 15 minutes or until peppers are blistered on all sides and onions are lightly browned, turning every few minutes. Remove from oven, place peppers in a bowl, cover with plastic wrap and let cool. Separate onion slices into rings and set aside.

Peel, stem and seed peppers, reserving juices. Slice three of the peppers into 3/4-inch strips. Place one pepper, the reserved juices, and 1/2 teaspoon thyme in blender or food processor and purée.

Heat oil in a large skillet over medium heat. Add escarole, salt, pepper and remaining 1/4 teaspoon thyme. Sauté until escarole is wilted, about 5 minutes.

Place 3 of the lasagna noodles on the bottom of a 9 x 13-inch baking dish. Cover with half of the escarole, 1 tablespoon Parmesan, half the pepper strips and onion rings. Repeat layer. Spread half the purée over the top and cover with the last noodles. Top with the remaining purée, 2 tablespoons Parmesan and Gorgonzola.

Bake at 350° for 30 minutes. Let stand 10 minutes before serving.

Serves 6

This is a wonderful side dish or a great vegetarian meal!

FISH & SEAFOOD

Salmon en Papillote
122

Grilled Salmon with Yogurt Dill Sauce
123

Barbecue Butter for Fish
123

Salmon in Phyllo
124

Salmon with Ginger Butter
125

Sauced Shrimp
125

Shrimp in Phyllo
126

Ginger Garlic Shrimp
127

Indian Spiced Shrimp
128

Catch & Keep Grilled Trout
129

Pacific Fresh Cioppino
130

Caribbean Snapper
131

Moroccan Fish
131

Baked White Fish with Pesto
132

Scallops with Asparagus in Parchment
132

Sun-Dried Scallop Sauté
133

Golden Tequila Sauce for White Fish
133

Crab Stuffed Sole
134

Seasoned Stuffed Sole
135

Grilled Mahi Mahi with Mango Salsa
136

Ginger Halibut in Parchment
137

Photo: Catch & Keep Grilled Trout

Salmon en Papillote

1 tablespoon butter

1 medium carrot, julienne sliced

1 leek, julienne sliced

   parchment paper

1 tablespoon olive oil

2 (8-ounce) salmon fillets, skin
   removed

1/4 teaspoon salt

1/8 teaspoon black pepper

1 small plum tomato, chopped

2 tablespoons fresh tarragon,
   stems removed and chopped

2 tablespoons clam juice

2 tablespoons dry white wine
   or vermouth

2 tablespoons lemon juice

Melt butter in a skillet over medium heat. Add carrots and leeks and sauté until tender but not soft, about 5 minutes.

Cut two 12 x 16-inch heart-shaped pieces of parchment paper and brush with olive oil. Place vegetables on one side of each piece of parchment. Place salmon fillets on top of vegetables and lightly season with salt and pepper. Top with tomato and tarragon. Combine clam juice, wine and lemon juice and pour over salmon. Fold paper over and seal by double folding all the edges.

Place on ungreased baking sheet and bake at 425° until fish flakes easily with a fork, about 15 minutes. Place individual packets on serving plate. Cut an X-shaped slit on top and fold back to serve.

Serves 2

> *When cooking en papillote (in a paper packet), steam builds up inside the package to cook the contents without any loss of nutrients. Flavors mingle to create delicately and distinctly flavored dishes.*

Grilled Salmon with Yogurt Dill Sauce

2 cups plain non-fat yogurt

1 tablespoon lemon juice

2 cloves garlic, minced

1 tablespoon fresh dill, chopped,
   or 1 teaspoon dried

1/8 teaspoon salt

1/8 teaspoon black pepper

   dash of hot pepper sauce

1/2 cucumber, peeled and
   thinly sliced

6 (8-ounce) salmon steaks
   or fillets

Combine yogurt with lemon juice, garlic, dill, salt, pepper and hot pepper sauce. Gently stir in cucumber.

Grill salmon over medium-hot coals until fish flakes easily, 10 to 20 minutes.

Spread yogurt dill sauce over salmon and serve.

Serves 6

It is best to grill fish in pieces weighing about eight ounces each. Smaller pieces are too thin to remain moist in the center.

Barbecue Butter for Fish

1/2 cup butter, softened

2 tablespoons lemon juice,
   freshly squeezed

1/2 teaspoon dried basil

1 teaspoon dried dill

1/2 teaspoon salt

1/4 teaspoon cayenne pepper

Beat all ingredients together with a mixer. Refrigerate for at least 2 hours to blend flavors. Spread butter generously on fish before barbecuing. (Prepared butter may be frozen.)

Makes 1/2 cup

Salmon in Phyllo

8 ounces fresh spinach,
rinsed and stemmed

1 cup watercress,
rinsed and stemmed

6 tablespoons sour cream,
divided

1/4 teaspoon salt

1/8 teaspoon black pepper

16 (12 x 16-inch) sheets phyllo
dough, thawed

6 tablespoons butter, melted and
cooled to room temperature

4 (6-ounce) salmon fillets,
skin removed

additional salt and pepper to
taste

4 teaspoons fresh dill, finely
chopped, or 1 teaspoon dried,
divided

Place spinach and watercress in a saucepan over medium heat and stir until wilted, about 3 minutes. Drain well, squeeze out remaining water and coarsely chop. Stir in 2 tablespoons sour cream, salt and pepper.

Unroll phyllo and cover with a damp towel. Place one sheet on a flat surface and brush with butter. Repeat with three additional sheets, placing them on top of each other. Fold the phyllo in half to create an 8 x 12-inch stack of phyllo. With the short end facing you, spread one fourth of the spinach mixture over the center of the bottom half of the phyllo. Place 1 salmon fillet on top of spinach, season with salt and pepper to taste and top with 1 tablespoon sour cream and 1 teaspoon fresh dill. Fold top half over bottom and lightly press edges together. (Edges may be trimmed prior to folding to form a fish shape, heart, or oval, if desired.) Repeat with remaining ingredients to make 3 more packets.

Bake at 375° on a lightly buttered baking sheet for 12 to 18 minutes, or until golden brown.

Serves 4

Salmon with Ginger Butter

3 tablespoons dry sherry

2 tablespoons soy sauce

1 tablespoon sesame oil

1 tablespoon fresh ginger, minced

2 pounds salmon fillets

2 tablespoons fresh parsley, chopped

2 tablespoons butter, cut into small pieces

1/8 teaspoon salt

1/8 teaspoon black pepper

Combine sherry, soy sauce, oil and ginger. Brush fillets with sherry mixture and sprinkle with parsley. Dot butter evenly across surface. Season with salt and pepper. (May be prepared several hours ahead to this point. Cover and refrigerate.)

Broil or grill salmon, without turning, until fish turns pink and flakes easily, approximately 10 minutes.

Serves 4

To prevent fish from sticking to the grill rack, be sure it is clean and very hot before placing the fish on it.

Sauced Shrimp

24 large prawns with shells

3 tablespoons all-purpose flour

6 tablespoons butter

1/2 cup brandy

1/2 cup Amaretto

1/3 cup dry white wine

3 oranges, halved

6 tablespoons whipping cream

1 1/2 tablespoons orange zest

1 cup white rice, cooked

Slit prawns from inner curve to butterfly. Dust lightly with flour. Melt butter in a large skillet over medium-high heat until bubbly. Add prawns and sauté 4 minutes per side. Transfer to heated platter and keep warm.

Increase heat and add brandy, Amaretto and wine. Squeeze juice from oranges directly into skillet, stirring constantly. Add cream and zest and continue stirring until thoroughly blended. Return prawns to pan and heat through, about 2 minutes. Serve over white rice.

Serves 4

Shrimp in Phyllo

Scampi Butter

> 1 **cup butter, softened**
>
> 1/2 **teaspoon paprika**
>
> 1 **teaspoon fresh parsley, chopped**
>
> 1 **teaspoon garlic, minced**
>
> 1/4 **teaspoon salt**
>
> 1/8 **teaspoon black pepper**

Shrimp

> 12 **(12 x 16-inch) sheets phyllo dough, thawed**
>
> **olive oil**
>
> 36 **shrimp (16 - 20 per pound), peeled and deveined**
>
> **lemon wedges**

Mix Scampi Butter ingredients until thoroughly combined. Set aside.

Unroll phyllo and cover with a damp towel. Lay one sheet on a flat work surface and brush lightly with olive oil. Repeat with two additional sheets. Slice the stacked sheets lengthwise into three equal pieces.

Place three shrimp and 1/2 to 1 tablespoon Scampi Butter on the corner of each pastry stack. Fold to form a triangle as if folding a flag. Brush triangle with olive oil just before last fold to help secure the wrap. Repeat until all shrimp are wrapped.

Place triangles seam side down in jelly roll pan and bake at 375° until golden brown, about 17 minutes. Serve with lemon wedges.

Serves 6

> *These packets can easily be made into small elegant appetizers!*

Ginger Garlic Shrimp

Marinade

- 1 tablespoon sesame oil
- 1 tablespoon garlic, minced
- 1 tablespoon fresh ginger, minced
- 1/4 teaspoon crushed red pepper
- 1 tablespoon soy sauce

Shrimp

- 16 ounces uncooked shrimp, peeled and deveined
- 2 teaspoons cornstarch
- 1/2 cup chicken broth
- 1/4 cup rice wine vinegar
- 2 tablespoons sugar
- 2 tablespoons soy sauce
- 6 green onions, cut into 1/2-inch pieces
- 1 cup snow peas
- 1 cup red bell pepper, julienne sliced
- cooked white rice

Combine marinade ingredients. Add shrimp and let stand 15 minutes.

Place cornstarch in a small bowl and gradually add chicken broth, stirring until cornstarch dissolves. Add vinegar, sugar and 2 tablespoons soy sauce.

Heat a wok or large, heavy skillet over high heat, add shrimp with marinade, onions, snow peas and pepper. Stir-fry until shrimp is pink, about 3 minutes. Add cornstarch mixture and stir until sauce thickens, about 1 minute. Serve with rice.

Serves 4

Deveining shrimp is a simple procedure. Place the peeled shrimp on a cutting board and use a sharp paring knife to make a shallow cut down the back of the shrimp exposing the "vein". Pull the vein out while rinsing under cold water.

Indian Spiced Shrimp

1 tablespoon olive oil

1 1/2 pounds large shrimp, peeled and deveined

1/8 teaspoon crushed red pepper

1/4 teaspoon salt

1/8 teaspoon freshly ground black pepper

2 tablespoons shallots, minced

5 large cloves garlic, minced

1 1/2 tablespoons fresh ginger, minced

1/2 teaspoon ground cumin

2 teaspoons curry

1 (28-ounce) can plum tomatoes with juice, chopped

1 cup red bell pepper (about 1), thinly sliced

1 cup green bell pepper (about 1), thinly sliced

1 1/2 cups zucchini (about 1 medium), halved lengthwise and cut into 1/2-inch slices

4 green onions, sliced into 2-inch lengths

1/4 cup fresh cilantro, chopped, or 1 tablespoon dried

1 tablespoon lemon juice

1 cup white rice, cooked

Heat oil in a large skillet over medium-high heat. Add shrimp, red pepper, salt and pepper. Sauté for 2 to 3 minutes or until shrimp turns bright pink. Use a slotted spoon to transfer shrimp to a plate.

Add shallots, garlic, ginger, cumin and curry to the skillet. Sauté until shallots are lightly browned, about 1 minute. Stir in tomatoes, peppers, zucchini and onions. Cook over medium heat, stirring frequently until the sauce has slightly thickened, about 8 minutes. Add shrimp, cilantro and lemon juice to the skillet, heat through and serve over cooked rice.

Serves 6

One cup of raw white rice yields about 3 cups cooked.

Catch & Keep Grilled Trout

5 tablespoons butter, softened and divided

1/2 cup celery, chopped

3/4 cup leeks, chopped

2 tablespoons shallots, chopped

1 1/2 tablespoons garlic, minced

1 1/2 cups unseasoned cornbread stuffing, crushed

1 1/2 teaspoons dried tarragon

1/2 teaspoon dried dill

1/4 teaspoon cayenne pepper

1/2 teaspoon salt

1 cup baby shrimp, cooked

1 egg, beaten

4 (8-ounce) whole trout, rinsed and patted dry

2 tablespoons butter, melted

4 tablespoons lemon juice, freshly squeezed

1 (6-ounce) package dried corn husks, soaked in water for 30 minutes

lemon slices and fresh dill, for garnish, optional

Melt 3 tablespoons butter in a large skillet. Add celery, leeks and shallots and sauté until just tender, about 20 minutes. Add garlic, sauté for 2 minutes and remove from heat.

Combine cornbread crumbs, tarragon, dill, cayenne and salt in a large bowl. Add celery mixture, shrimp, egg and remaining 2 tablespoons butter. Combine well.

Stuff each trout with 1 cup stuffing mixture. Drizzle each trout with 1/2 tablespoon melted butter and 1 tablespoon lemon juice. Wrap each stuffed trout with corn husks to completely cover fish with 2 layers of husks. Secure corn husks in 3 places by tying with kitchen string that has been soaked in water.

Place on a covered grill for 18 to 22 minutes or bake at 400° for 20 minutes. Fish is done when it flakes easily with a fork. Garnish with lemon and dill, if desired.

Serves 4

When storing whole fish for more than a few hours, dip it in a bowl of cold water with a squeeze of lemon. Carefully pat dry and refrigerate in the coldest part of your refrigerator.

Pacific Fresh Cioppino

3 tablespoons olive oil

1½ cups onion, chopped

2 cloves garlic, minced

1 cup green pepper, chopped

1 (28-ounce) can tomatoes with juice, slightly puréed

1 (16-ounce) can tomato sauce

1 cup dry white wine or clam juice

½ teaspoon dried thyme

¼ teaspoon dried basil

¼ teaspoon dried oregano

1 bay leaf

1 teaspoon salt

¼ teaspoon freshly ground black pepper

1½ pounds white fish (such as snapper or cod), cut into ½-inch pieces

8 ounces medium shrimp, shelled and deveined

16-20 steamer clams, scrubbed

2 (3 to 4-pound) dungeness crabs, cooked, cleaned and cracked

¼ cup fresh parsley, chopped

Heat oil in a large stock pot over medium heat. Sauté onion, garlic and green pepper until tender, about 3 minutes. Add tomatoes, tomato sauce, wine, herbs, salt and pepper. Cover and simmer for 15 minutes.

Add fish and shrimp and simmer an additional 10 minutes, covered, being careful not to boil. Add clams and cracked crab (in the shell) and cook until clams open, about 5 minutes. Discard any clams that do not open. Remove bay leaf, stir in parsley and serve.

Serves 6 to 8

Leaving the crab in the shell makes an attractive presentation, however taking it out of the shell before cooking makes this dish easier to eat.

FISH & SEAFOOD

Caribbean Snapper

3 pounds red snapper fillets

1/2 cup shallots, chopped

4 cloves garlic, minced

1/4 cup freshly squeezed lime juice

1 cup orange juice

1/4 cup dark rum

1 cup dry white wine

1/4 cup soy sauce

2 teaspoons dried rosemary

1/4 cup fresh parsley, chopped

1/4 teaspoon white pepper

1/4 teaspoon salt

Place fillets in a covered container or ziplock bag. Combine remaining ingredients and pour over fillets. Refrigerate for 2 to 8 hours.

Remove fish from marinade and pour marinade into a medium saucepan. Bring to a boil and cook until reduced by half, about 12 minutes.

Grill or broil fish for 3 to 4 minutes on each side according to thickness. Spoon sauce over fish and serve immediately.

Serves 6

Try this recipe with any firm white fish, such as halibut or cod.

Moroccan Fish

1 1/2 pounds red snapper fillets

6 cloves garlic, crushed

1 1/4 teaspoons salt

1 1/2 teaspoons paprika

1 1/2 teaspoons cumin

1/2 teaspoon cayenne pepper

1/2 cup fresh cilantro, chopped

2 tablespoons lemon juice

Place fish in a shallow dish. Combine remaining ingredients, pour over fish and marinate for at least one hour.

Remove fish from marinade and bake, uncovered, at 400° until fish flakes easily with a fork, about 10 minutes per inch of thickness.

Serves 4

Properly cooked fish has opaque flesh, while undercooked fish will appear slightly translucent.

Baked White Fish with Pesto

4 **(5 to 6 ounce) skinless white fish fillets such as cod, halibut, roughy or snapper**

2 **tablespoons olive oil**

1/4 **cup basil pesto**

1/2 **cup mayonnaise**

1 **teaspoon lemon juice**

Rinse fillets and pat dry. Place fish in a baking dish that has been coated with olive oil.

Combine pesto, mayonnaise and lemon juice and spread over fillets. Bake at 425° until fish flakes easily with a fork, about 8 minutes.

Serves 4

A recipe for Basil Pesto can be found on page 105.

Scallops with Asparagus in Parchment

1 **medium red bell pepper, sliced into 1/4-inch strips**

1 **pound fresh asparagus, ends trimmed and cut into 3-inch pieces**

parchment paper

1 1/2 **pounds small bay scallops (or larger, cut in half)**

3 **tablespoons butter**

1/4 **cup all-purpose flour**

1/4 **teaspoon salt**

1/4 **teaspoon black pepper**

1 **cup milk**

6 **tablespoons dry sherry**

1/4 **cup Parmesan cheese, grated**

Steam or microwave red pepper and asparagus until tender-crisp. Cut six 13 x 12-inch heart-shaped pieces of parchment paper. Arrange asparagus and red pepper on one half of each heart. Divide scallops and place on top of vegetables.

Melt butter over medium heat in a small saucepan. Stir in flour, salt and pepper and cook until bubbly. Gradually add milk and sherry and cook until mixture boils and thickens, stirring constantly. Spoon sauce over scallops and sprinkle with Parmesan. Fold paper over and seal by double folding all the edges. Place on an ungreased baking sheet and bake at 425° for 10 minutes. Let stand 5 minutes. Place individual packets on serving plate. Cut an X-shaped slit on top and fold back to serve.

Serves 6

Sun-Dried Scallop Sauté

1 1/2 tablespoons olive oil

12 ounces large sea scallops

1/4 cup oil-packed sun-dried tomatoes

3/4 cup dry white wine

1/3 cup whipping cream

2 tablespoons butter, softened

1 tablespoon garlic, minced

1/4 teaspoon salt

1/8 teaspoon black pepper

Heat oil in a large, heavy skillet over high heat. Add scallops and sauté until brown and cooked through, about 2 minutes per side. Transfer scallops to plates, and keep warm.

Drain and thinly slice tomatoes. Add wine and tomatoes to skillet. Cook and stir 2 minutes, scraping up any brown bits. Add cream and boil until mixture is reduced to sauce consistency, about 2 minutes.

Remove sauce from heat, add butter and garlic and whisk until melted. Season with salt and pepper. Pour over scallops and serve immediately.

Serves 2

Golden Tequila Sauce for White Fish

zest and juice of 1 small lime

1/2 cup tomato, seeded and diced

4 green onions, thinly sliced

1 tablespoon tequila

1/2 teaspoon salt, divided

1/4 teaspoon pepper, divided

1 to 2 tablespoons butter

1/4 cup all-purpose flour

1 pound firm white fish

Combine lime juice, tomato, onions, tequila, 1/4 teaspoon salt and 1/8 teaspoon pepper in a bowl. Cover and refrigerate for 2 to 3 hours.

Heat butter in an oven-proof sauté pan. Season flour with remaining 1/4 teaspoon salt and 1/8 teaspoon pepper. Lightly flour the fish and brown on one side. Turn fish over, cover with tequila sauce and bake at 350° for 10 to 15 minutes or until fish flakes in the center. Top fish with lime zest and serve immediately.

Serves 2

If you don't have a citrus zester, remove the outer peel of the lime and slice it into very thin strips.

Grilled Mahi Mahi with Mango Salsa

Salsa

- 3 tablespoons lime juice
- 1 tablespoon fish sauce or fish extract
- 1 teaspoon sugar
- 2 tablespoons green onions, sliced
- 2 tablespoons fresh cilantro, chopped
- 2 ripe but firm mangos, peeled and diced
- 1 cup Walla Walla or other sweet onions, chopped
- 1½ cups tomatoes, chopped
- 1 or 2 jalapeño peppers, chopped, or 1 teaspoon crushed red pepper
- 1 teaspoon garlic, minced

Fish

- 2 pounds Mahi Mahi

Combine lime juice, fish sauce and sugar in a large bowl. Stir until sugar dissolves. Add remaining salsa ingredients, mix, cover and refrigerate for 30 minutes. Stir well before serving.

Grill Mahi Mahi over medium-hot coals until fish flakes easily, about 15 minutes. Serve salsa over fish.

Serves 4

Fish sauce can be found in the International section of many supermarkets. Try this recipe with any firm white fish such as halibut, cod or red snapper.

Ginger Halibut in Parchment

Marinade

3 tablespoons soy sauce

1 tablespoon olive oil

1 clove garlic, minced

1 tablespoon fresh ginger, grated

Fish

4 (6 to 8-ounce) halibut fillets, less than 1-inch thick

parchment paper or aluminum foil

1 cup (about 3 ounces) snow peas, trimmed

1 small red bell pepper, cut into julienne strips

1 cup carrots (about 1 medium), peeled and cut into julienne strips

1/3 cup green onions, chopped

Combine marinade ingredients and place in a shallow dish. Add fish and marinate for 10 minutes.

Cut four 20 x 16-inch heart-shaped pieces of parchment paper. Combine the snow peas, pepper, carrots and onions. Place one-fourth of the vegetables on one side of each piece of parchment. Place fillets on top of vegetables. Spoon marinade over fillets. Fold paper over and seal by double folding all of the edges.

Place on an ungreased cookie sheet and bake at 375° until fish flakes easily with a fork, about 15 minutes. Place individual packets on a serving plate. Cut an X-shaped slit on top and fold back to serve.

Serves 4

These delicious packets can be prepared early in the day and refrigerated prior to baking.

POULTRY

Chicken Breasts with
Apple Cream Sauce
140

Herbed Chicken Fricassee
141

Smothered Chicken
142

Cypress Chicken and Rice
143

No-Fuss Chicken
144

Open Sesame Chicken
144

Camp Jack Chicken
145

Balsamic Grilled Chicken Breasts
146

Buffy's Favorite Chicken
146

Lime Grilled Jalapeño Chicken
147

Chicken and Cheese Enchiladas
147

River Road Burritos
with Avocado Salsa
148

Southwestern Grilled
Chicken Sandwiches
149

A Perfect Ten
150

Spicy Ginger Garlic Chicken
151

Mexican Skillet Chicken
151

Five Spice Stir-Fry
152

Fiery Thai Style Pizza
153

Rick's Radio Roasted Chicken
154

Palouse Pheasant
with Mushroom Sauce
155

Black Bean and Turkey Stew
156

The Great Turkey Caper
157

Turkey Tidbits
157

Photo: Lime Grilled Jalapeño Chicken, Mexican Black Beans with Rice and Avocado Salsa

Chicken Breasts with Apple Cream Sauce

4 boneless chicken breast halves, skinned

1/4 cup all-purpose flour

3 tablespoons olive oil

1/3 cup white onion, thinly sliced

1/3 cup Granny Smith apple, peeled and julienne sliced

2 cloves garlic, crushed

1/2 cup chardonnay or other dry white wine

1/2 teaspoon lemon juice

3 tablespoons golden raisins

1/4 teaspoon salt

1/4 teaspoon freshly ground black pepper

1 tablespoon fresh rosemary, chopped, or 1 teaspoon dried

1/2 cup whipping cream

1/4 cup pecans, chopped and toasted

Dredge chicken in flour. Heat oil over medium heat in a heavy skillet with a lid. Brown chicken in oil, about 2 minutes per side. Remove to platter and keep warm.

In the same pan sauté onion, apple and garlic until soft, about 4 minutes. Reduce heat to medium and add wine, lemon juice, raisins, salt and pepper. Simmer, uncovered, for 5 minutes.

Add rosemary and cream to the apple mixture, stirring until blended. Return chicken to the pan, cover and cook for 10 minutes or until chicken is tender and cooked through. Remove chicken to serving dish and keep warm. Reduce sauce slightly by cooking for an additional 2 to 3 minutes. Pour sauce over chicken and sprinkle with toasted pecans.

Serves 4

Toasting pecans is easy in a microwave. Simply place them in a microwave-safe dish and cook on high for 3 to 4 minutes, stirring after each minute.

Herbed Chicken Fricassee

6 cloves garlic, chopped

2/3 cup mixed fresh herbs, finely
chopped (marjoram, thyme,
sage, rosemary and savory)

2 tablespoons plus 3 teaspoons
olive oil, divided

2 tablespoons balsamic
or red wine vinegar

6 chicken thighs, skinned

3 large chicken breast halves,
skinned

1/2 teaspoon salt

1/4 teaspoon black pepper

4 cups onion (about 3 medium
onions), chopped

1 1/2 tablespoons all-purpose flour

1 cup dry white wine

2 tablespoons tomato paste

4 cups low-fat chicken broth

1/4 cup fresh parsley, minced

cooked white rice

Combine garlic and herbs. Blend in 2 tablespoons oil and vinegar. Place chicken thighs and breasts in a large baking pan. Spread herb mixture over all sides of the chicken, cover and refrigerate for 4 to 24 hours.

Scrape herb mixture off chicken and reserve. Season chicken with salt and pepper. Heat 1 teaspoon oil in a large Dutch oven over medium heat. Cook chicken in batches, turning as necessary until all pieces are brown, adding remaining oil if necessary. Transfer chicken to a platter.

Sauté onion in Dutch oven until tender, about 5 minutes. Sprinkle flour over onion and cook for 1 minute, stirring constantly. Add wine and tomato paste and bring to a boil, scraping up any brown bits. Continue boiling until mixture is reduced by half, about 3 minutes. Return chicken and reserved herb mixture to Dutch oven, add chicken broth. Cover and simmer until tender, about 20 minutes.

Transfer chicken back to the platter and cover. Bring cooking liquid to a boil and cook until reduced to sauce consistency, about 25 minutes. Return chicken to Dutch oven, add parsley and re-heat. Serve over rice.

Serves 6

If you need to chop both garlic and fresh herbs, do them together. The garlic will stick to the herbs instead of the knife!

Smothered Chicken

1/4 cup all-purpose flour

1/2 teaspoon paprika

1 teaspoon salt

6 to 8 chicken breasts and thighs (about 2½ pounds), skinned

vegetable cooking spray

1 teaspoon vegetable oil

2 cups onion, thinly sliced and separated into rings

1 (2½-ounce) package dry chicken noodle soup mix

3/4 cup water

1 (12-ounce) can evaporated skim milk

1/4 cup fresh parsley, chopped, optional

Combine flour, paprika and salt in a shallow bowl. Dredge chicken pieces in flour mixture and set aside.

Spray a large skillet with cooking spray. Add oil and heat to medium. Add chicken and cook until evenly browned, about 3 minutes per side. Scatter onion rings and soup mix over chicken and stir in water. Cover tightly, reduce heat and simmer until chicken is tender and cooked through, about 35 minutes.

Remove chicken to a platter and keep warm. Stir milk and parsley into skillet. Cook until thoroughly heated and slightly thickened, about 3 minutes. Pour sauce over chicken and serve.

Serves 6

Rice is the perfect accompaniment for this chicken recipe that pleases children and adults alike.

Cypress Chicken and Rice

1 tablespoon vegetable oil

8 chicken thighs, skinned

1 cup long grain rice, uncooked

3/4 cup onion, chopped

4 cloves garlic, finely chopped

1 cup chicken broth, divided

2 (14 1/2-ounce) cans tomatoes
   with liquid

3 tablespoons fresh oregano,
   chopped, or 3 teaspoons dried

1 tablespoon fresh thyme,
   chopped, or 1 teaspoon dried

12 Kalamata or black olives,
   pitted and quartered

1 ounce (about 1/4 cup)
   feta cheese, crumbled

Heat oil in a Dutch oven over medium-high heat. Add half of the thighs and cook until they are browned, about 4 minutes per side. Remove to a platter and repeat with remaining thighs.

Reduce heat to medium and add rice, onion, garlic and 1/4 cup of broth. Cook, stirring constantly, until onion is soft, about 4 minutes. Add remaining broth, tomatoes, oregano and thyme. Press the thighs into the rice mixture and bring to a boil. Cover, reduce heat and simmer until rice is tender, 20 to 30 minutes.

Stir the olives into the chicken and rice and sprinkle cheese on top. Serve immediately.

Serves 8

Olives are high in fiber, vitamin A, iron and sodium. Their flavor is deep and rich - a few go a long way!

No-Fuss Chicken

aluminum foil or
parchment paper

4 boneless chicken breast halves,
skinned

3 tablespoons Dijon mustard

1/4 cup all-purpose flour

2 teaspoons vegetable oil

1 cup fresh mushrooms, sliced

1/4 cup green onions, sliced

4 teaspoons butter

4 tablespoons soy sauce

Cut four pieces of aluminum foil into 12-inch squares. Brush each side of the chicken with mustard and dredge in flour. Place each chicken breast on one piece of foil.

Heat oil in a medium skillet. Add mushrooms and onions and sauté for 5 minutes or until mushrooms are tender. Remove from heat, and place one quarter of the vegetables on top of each chicken breast. Top each breast with 1 teaspoon butter and 1 tablespoon soy sauce.

Fold foil over chicken and seal edges well, leaving a "tent" above chicken. Bake at 350° for 25 minutes. May be prepared ahead of time and refrigerated prior to baking.

Serves 4

Great with rice, these individual packets are a do-ahead party hit!

Open Sesame Chicken

2 tablespoons all-purpose flour

2 tablespoons sesame seeds

1/4 teaspoon salt

2 tablespoons soy sauce

4 large chicken breast halves,
skinned

2 tablespoons butter, melted

Combine flour, sesame seeds and salt in a shallow dish. Dip chicken in soy sauce and then dredge in flour mixture. Place flesh side up in a baking dish and drizzle with melted butter.

Bake at 400°, basting occasionally, for 40 minutes or until tender.

Serves 4

Camp Jack Chicken

8 to 10 chicken thighs and breasts, rinsed and patted dry

1 teaspoon garlic salt

1 teaspoon black pepper

2 tablespoons olive oil

1 tablespoon dried tarragon

1 clove garlic, minced

1 cup morel, chanterelle or cultivated mushrooms, sliced

1/2 cup green onions, chopped

1 cup dry white wine

1/2 cup white wine vinegar

cooked rice

Season chicken with garlic salt and pepper. Heat oil in a large, heavy skillet over medium-high heat. Add chicken and sauté until golden brown. Remove to a platter and cover with foil.

Add tarragon, garlic, mushrooms and onions to skillet and sauté for 1 minute. Stir in wine and vinegar and bring to a boil for 1 minute. Return chicken to skillet, cover, reduce heat and simmer for 45 minutes.

Transfer chicken to a platter and cover with foil. Bring sauce to a boil and reduce until slightly thickened. Remove mushrooms and onions with a slotted spoon. Pour half the sauce over the chicken and garnish with mushrooms and onions. Serve remaining sauce over rice.

Serves 6 to 8

Experiment with a combination of fresh and reconstituted wild mushrooms in this recipe. It is one of the best ways to intensify the deep, woodsy flavor of wild mushrooms.

Balsamic Grilled Chicken Breasts

6 boneless chicken breast halves, skinned

2 tablespoons olive oil

1/4 cup balsamic vinegar

5 teaspoons sugar

5 teaspoons catsup

1 1/2 teaspoons Worcestershire sauce

1 green onion, minced

1/2 teaspoon dry mustard

1/4 teaspoon garlic, minced

1/4 teaspoon salt

1/4 teaspoon black pepper

2 drops hot pepper sauce

Place the chicken in a covered container or ziplock bag. Combine remaining ingredients and pour over chicken. Refrigerate for 4 to 24 hours, turning occasionally.

Remove chicken from marinade and grill over medium coals for 4 minutes. Turn chicken and grill until chicken is cooked through but still moist, about 3 minutes.

Serves 6

Balsamic vinegar has become increasingly popular because of its sweet pungency without the sharp acidity of lighter vinegars.

Buffy's Favorite Chicken

3 pounds chicken pieces

1/4 cup vegetable oil

1/2 cup soy sauce

1/4 cup sauterne wine or sherry

2 teaspoons ground ginger

2 teaspoons dry mustard

1 clove garlic, chopped

Remove skin from chicken pieces and place in a covered container or ziplock bag. Combine remaining ingredients and pour over chicken. Refrigerate for 1 to 24 hours, turning occasionally.

Remove chicken from marinade. Grill over medium-low coals. Turn and baste with marinade frequently until done, about 45 minutes.

Serves 4 to 6

Lime Grilled Jalapeño Chicken

4 boneless chicken breasts
halves, skinned

¹/4 cup olive oil

¹/2 cup fresh lime juice

1¹/2 teaspoons garlic powder

2 tablespoons jalapeño pepper,
seeded and minced

¹/4 teaspoon salt

¹/8 teaspoon black pepper

Place each chicken breast between 2 sheets of waxed paper and pound to 1/4-inch thickness. Combine oil, lime juice, garlic powder and jalapeño pepper and pour into a covered container or ziplock bag. Add chicken and marinate 1 to 2 hours, turning occasionally. Remove chicken and reserve marinade. Season chicken with salt and pepper. Grill over medium-hot coals for 5 minutes on each side, basting twice with marinade during grilling.

Serves 4

Chicken and Cheese Enchiladas

1 tablespoon butter

1 cup onion, chopped

1¹/2 cups cooked chicken, shredded

2 cups picanté sauce, divided

4 ounces cream cheese

1 teaspoon ground cumin

2 cups sharp cheddar cheese,
shredded and divided

8 to 10 (6-inch) flour tortillas

Melt butter in a large skillet over medium heat. Add onion and sauté until tender, about 3 minutes. Stir in chicken, 1/2 cup picanté sauce, cream cheese and cumin. Cook until thoroughly heated. Add 1 cup cheese and remove from heat.

Spoon 1 cup picanté sauce on the bottom of a greased 9 x 13-inch baking dish. Spoon approximately 1/4 cup chicken mixture into the center of each tortilla, roll and place seam-side down in pan. Top with remaining picanté sauce and cheese.

Cover with foil and bake at 325° for 20 minutes. Remove foil and bake for an additional 10 minutes.

Serves 4 to 6

River Road Burritos with Avocado Salsa

1/2 cup olive oil, divided

1 1/2 cups red onion,
chopped and divided

1 (4 1/2-ounce) can chopped
green chilies, divided

2 1/2 teaspoons chili powder,
divided

1 1/4 teaspoons ground cumin,
divided

1 1/2 teaspoons salt, divided

2 (16-ounce) cans black beans,
rinsed and drained

6 tablespoons lime juice, divided

1 1/2 pounds boneless chicken
breasts, skinned and cut into
3/4-inch pieces

1 large avocado, diced

1 large tomato, seeded and diced

1/2 cup cilantro leaves, divided

6 burrito-sized flour tortillas

4 cups romaine lettuce, rinsed
and thinly sliced

salt and black pepper to taste

3/4 cup goat cheese, crumbled

Heat 2 tablespoons oil in a saucepan over medium heat. Add 1 cup onion and sauté until tender, about 8 minutes. Add 3 tablespoons chilies, 1 teaspoon chili powder, 1/2 teaspoon cumin and 1 teaspoon salt. Stir in beans and 2 tablespoons lime juice. Cook and stir, mashing beans slightly with a spoon, until heated through, about 4 minutes. Remove from heat.

Heat 2 tablespoons oil in a large skillet over high heat. Add chicken and cook until almost cooked through, about 3 minutes. Stir in 1 1/2 teaspoons chili powder and 3/4 teaspoon cumin. Cook for 2 more minutes. Remove from heat.

To make the avocado salsa, combine avocado, tomato, 1/2 cup onion, 3 tablespoons green chilies, 2 tablespoons oil, 1/2 teaspoon salt and 2 tablespoons lime juice. Chop 1/4 cup cilantro leaves and stir in. Set aside.

To assemble the burritos, wrap tortillas in foil and bake at 325° until warm, about 5 minutes. Combine lettuce, 1/4 cup whole cilantro leaves, 2 tablespoons oil and 2 tablespoons lime juice. Season with salt and pepper and toss. Place tortillas on a flat surface and spread with 1/2 cup bean mixture. Sprinkle with 2 tablespoons goat cheese, 2/3 cup lettuce, 1/3 cup chicken and roll up.

Place each burrito seam side down on a plate and top with 1/3 cup salsa.

Serves 6

Southwestern Grilled Chicken Sandwiches

Cilantro Pesto

- 2 **large cloves garlic, peeled**
- 1 **cup loosely packed fresh cilantro, stems removed**
- 1/4 **teaspoon salt**
- 1/4 **teaspoon freshly ground black pepper**
- 1 **teaspoon water**
- 2 **teaspoons olive oil**
- 1/4 **cup Parmesan cheese, grated**
- 2 **tablespoons lemon juice**

Sandwich

- 4 **boneless chicken breast halves, skinned and pounded to 1/2-inch thickness**

  provolone cheese, optional *
- 4 **hamburger buns**

  mayonnaise, optional *
- 1 **tomato, sliced, optional**

Drop garlic into food processor while it is running and process until minced. Add remaining pesto ingredients and process until thoroughly blended.

Spread pesto over both sides of chicken. Cover and refrigerate for at least 2 hours. Grill chicken over medium-hot coals for 5 minutes per side or until done. If desired, top with cheese and melt. Serve on buns with mayonnaise and tomato, if desired.

Serves 4

> ** Lite 'n Hearty certification applies only when the optional cheese and mayonnaise are omitted.*

A Perfect Ten

Marinade

- 1/3 **cup soy sauce**
- 1/4 **cup fresh cilantro, chopped**
- 1/4 **cup green onions, chopped**
- 1/4 **cup chicken broth**
- 2 **tablespoons fresh ginger, peeled and chopped**
- 2 **tablespoons rice wine vinegar**
- 4 **cloves garlic, chopped**
- 2 **teaspoons hot chili paste with garlic**
- 1 **teaspoon sesame oil**

Chicken

- 6 **boneless chicken breast halves, skinned and pounded to 1/2-inch thickness**

Vegetables

- 1 1/3 **cups small carrots, thinly sliced on diagonal**
- 1 1/3 **cups jicama, peeled and cut into match sticks**
- 1 **cup snow peas**
- 2 **teaspoons sesame oil**
- 1 **tablespoon sesame seeds**
- 2 **tablespoons chicken broth**

Combine marinade ingredients. Pour 1/2 cup marinade into covered container or ziplock bag. Add chicken and refrigerate for 2 to 4 hours, turning occasionally. Reserve remaining marinade.

Bring a medium pot of salted water to a boil. Add carrots and simmer 3 minutes. Add jicama and peas and cook until just tender, about 2 minutes. Drain and rinse with cold water. (Can be prepared up to 4 hours in advance, cover and chill.)

Drain chicken. Heat 2 teaspoons sesame oil in a skillet over medium-high heat. Add chicken and cook 3 minutes. Turn chicken and sprinkle with sesame seeds. Pour in broth, cover and cook until chicken is cooked through, about 3 minutes. Place on a serving platter and keep warm.

Combine vegetables in a saucepan with reserved marinade. Cook until just heated through. Place vegetables on top of the chicken, drizzle juices over top and serve immediately.

Serves 6

Chili paste with garlic can be found in the International section of many supermarkets.

Spicy Ginger Garlic Chicken

8 boneless chicken breast halves

4 cloves garlic, minced

1½ teaspoons fresh ginger, peeled and grated

½ teaspoon salt

½ teaspoon crushed red pepper

¼ teaspoon black pepper

¼ teaspoon ground cinnamon

¼ teaspoon ground cardamom

1 tablespoon catsup

1 tablespoon red wine vinegar

1 teaspoon water

Remove skin from chicken breasts. Combine garlic, ginger, salt, red pepper, black pepper, cinnamon and cardamom in a small bowl. Stir in catsup, vinegar and water. Brush both sides of chicken with mixture. Place chicken in a shallow baking pan. Bake, uncovered, at 375° until no longer pink, about 20 minutes.

Serves 8

Mexican Skillet Chicken

4 boneless chicken breast halves

1 teaspoon chili powder

¼ teaspoon salt

¼ teaspoon black pepper

1 tablespoon vegetable oil

1 (15-ounce) can black beans

1 cup chunky tomato salsa

1 cup tomato, chopped

Remove skin from chicken breasts and set aside. Combine chili powder, salt and pepper and sprinkle evenly on both sides of the chicken. Heat oil in a large skillet over medium heat. Add chicken and cook 10 minutes, turning to brown both sides.

Rinse and drain beans. Stir in beans, salsa and tomato. Heat to boiling. Cover, reduce heat and simmer 3 to 5 minutes or until chicken is done and beans are thoroughly heated.

Serves 4

Five Spice Stir-Fry

1/4 cup plus 2 teaspoons all-purpose flour, divided

3/4 teaspoon Chinese five spice powder, divided

1 teaspoon salt

4 boneless chicken breast halves, skinned and cut into 1/4-inch strips

1 cup chicken broth

2 teaspoons sugar

1 tablespoon soy sauce

1/2 teaspoon sesame oil

1 teaspoon white vinegar

1 tablespoon sherry

1/4 teaspoon black pepper

1/2 cup vegetable oil

15 dried red chilies, seeded

2 cloves garlic, chopped

2 teaspoons fresh ginger, chopped

6 green onions, cut into 2-inch lengths

1 tablespoon water

1 cup white rice, cooked

Combine 1/4 cup flour, 1/2 teaspoon five spice powder and salt in a bowl. Toss chicken in flour mixture to coat and set aside. Combine broth, sugar, soy sauce, sesame oil, vinegar, sherry, pepper and remaining 1/4 teaspoon five spice powder in a bowl and set aside.

Heat vegetable oil in a wok or large skillet until very hot. Stir-fry chicken, one-third at a time, until brown on all sides and cooked through. Drain chicken on paper towels. Let oil return to high heat between batches, adding additional oil if necessary.

Pour off all but 2 tablespoons oil. Add chilies, garlic and ginger. Stir-fry until lightly browned and chilies are dark, 2 to 4 minutes. Add onions and stir-fry for a few seconds. Pour in broth mixture and bring to a boil. Combine remaining 2 teaspoons flour and 1 tablespoon water and add to wok. Stir constantly until sauce boils and thickens, about 4 to 6 minutes. Return chicken to wok and cook until thoroughly heated. Serve immediately over white rice.

Serves 4

Chinese five spice, found in the International section of most supermarkets, is a wonderful blend of fennel, anise, ginger, licorice, cinnamon and cloves. Try this recipe and discover a whole new range of flavors!

Fiery Thai Style Pizza

Sauce

- 3/4 **cup rice vinegar**
- 1/4 **cup brown sugar**
- 1/4 **cup soy sauce**
- 3 **tablespoons water**
- 2 **tablespoons peanut butter**
- 1 **tablespoon fresh ginger, peeled and minced**
- 1/2 **teaspoon crushed red pepper**
- 4 **cloves garlic, minced**

Pizza

- **vegetable cooking spray**
- 8 **ounces (about 2) boneless chicken breast halves, skinned and cut into 1/4-inch cubes**
- 1/4 **cup green onions, sliced**
- 1/2 **cup Swiss cheese, shredded**
- 1/4 **cup part-skim mozzarella cheese, shredded**
- 1 **(12-inch) pizza crust**

Combine sauce ingredients and set aside.

Coat a large non-stick skillet with cooking spray and sauté chicken over medium-high heat for 3 minutes. Remove from skillet and set aside.

Pour sauce into the skillet, bring to a boil and cook for 10 minutes or until mixture is reduced by half. Return chicken to skillet, add onions and cook for 2 minutes. Remove from heat.

Sprinkle cheeses over pizza crust and top with chicken mixture. Bake pizza at 500° for 10 to 12 minutes or until brown and cooked in the center.

Serves 4

If you love spicy food - you'll love this low-fat pizza!

Rick's Radio Roasted Chicken

1 whole roasting chicken, about
4 pounds, cleaned

2 tablespoons fresh rosemary,
chopped, or 2 teaspoons dried

2 tablespoons fresh thyme,
chopped, or 2 teaspoons dried

3/4 teaspoon salt

1 tablespoon coarsely ground
black pepper

4 to 6 medium cloves garlic,
peeled and slivered

Prepare chicken 4 to 24 hours before roasting. Combine rosemary, thyme, salt and pepper. Separate skin from the chicken's breast and thigh areas by running your fingers between the meat and the skin, being careful not to tear the skin, but to create a "pocket" between the meat and the skin. Rub seasoning mixture in the "pockets" and distribute the garlic slivers beneath the skin. Place any remaining seasonings and garlic in the cavity of chicken. (If the skin is torn, it may be sewn back together.) Place chicken in a covered container or plastic bag and refrigerate until ready to roast.

Preheat oven to 500°. Place chicken on a vertical roasting rack or breast side up in a roasting pan. Roast 35 to 45 minutes or until meat thermometer reads 190° degrees. Remove skin prior to serving.

Serves 4 to 6

Inspired by a commentator on a Public Radio talk program, this do-ahead chicken fills your kitchen with wonderful aromas. To avoid a smoking oven, be sure it's clean. Experiment with the recipe by substituting any of your favorite herbs!

Palouse Pheasant with Mushroom Sauce

Stuffing

- 2 tablespoons butter, melted
- 2 tablespoons bread crumbs
- 1 teaspoon fresh sage, chopped
- 1/2 teaspoon dry mustard
- 1/4 teaspoon salt
- 1/2 teaspoon black pepper

Pheasant

- 4 pheasant breasts with wings and skin on
- 1 tablespoon all-purpose flour
- 1 tablespoon butter
- 1 tablespoon olive oil

Sauce

- 2 tablespoons olive oil
- 2 tablespoons shallots, chopped
- 8 ounces chanterelle, shiitake or cultivated mushrooms, sliced
- 1 tablespoon all-purpose flour
- 1/4 cup dry white wine
- 1/4 cup chicken broth
- 1 tablespoon lemon juice
- 1/4 teaspoon paprika
- 1 teaspoon fresh sage, chopped
- 1/4 teaspoon cayenne pepper
- 1/4 teaspoon salt
- 1/4 teaspoon black pepper
- 1 tablespoon sherry

Combine stuffing ingredients. Make a small cut on the side of each breast, stuff with 1 tablespoon stuffing and pat closed. Dust breasts with 1 tablespoon flour.

Melt 1 tablespoon butter and 1 tablespoon oil in a heavy skillet over medium heat. Add pheasant breasts and cook on both sides until done, about 10 minutes. Remove breasts to a warm platter and cover.

For the sauce, add oil to the skillet and increase heat to medium-high. Add shallots and mushrooms and sauté until tender, about 4 minutes. Sprinkle flour over mushrooms and continue to sauté for 1 minute. Reduce heat to medium and add remaining sauce ingredients except sherry. Simmer until sauce thickens, about 3 minutes. Add sherry and heat through. Serve sauce over breasts.

Serves 4

You may substitute chicken breasts for the pheasant in this recipe. If so, double the bread crumb stuffing.

Black Bean and Turkey Stew

2 tablespoons vegetable oil, divided

1½ pounds boneless turkey breast, cut into ½-inch pieces

¾ teaspoon salt, divided

½ teaspoon freshly ground black pepper, divided

1 cup onion, chopped

2 tablespoons garlic, minced

½ teaspoon ground cumin

1 teaspoon chili powder

¼ teaspoon cinnamon

¼ teaspoon dried basil

¼ teaspoon crushed red pepper

¼ teaspoon ground sage

3 (15-ounce) cans black beans

1 (14½-ounce) can low-fat chicken broth

1 (4½-ounce) can chopped green chilies

1 cup frozen corn kernels, thawed

1 (7-ounce) jar roasted red peppers, drained and chopped

Cumin Topping

½ cup non-fat yogurt or sour cream

½ teaspoon ground cumin

¼ teaspoon salt

Heat 1 tablespoon oil in a Dutch oven over medium-high heat. Season turkey with 1/4 teaspoon salt and 1/4 teaspoon pepper. Cook turkey in small batches until golden brown on all sides, about 4 minutes. Remove to a platter and cover.

Add remaining 1 tablespoon oil to Dutch oven. Add onion and cook over medium heat for 2 minutes. Add garlic, remaining 1/2 teaspoon salt, 1/4 teaspoon pepper and spices. Cook for 1 minute and remove from heat.

Rinse and drain 1 can of beans and place in a blender. Add broth, purée until smooth and pour into Dutch oven. Rinse and drain remaining beans and stir into Dutch oven. Stir in chilies, corn and roasted peppers. Bring to a boil, reduce heat and simmer, uncovered, for 5 minutes. Return turkey to stew and heat through. Combine cumin topping ingredients and serve with stew.

Serves 4 to 6

The Great Turkey Caper

12 ounces boneless turkey cutlets

1/4 cup all-purpose flour

2 tablespoons vegetable oil, divided

2 large cloves garlic, minced

1 teaspoon cornstarch

1/4 cup dry white wine

1/2 cup chicken broth

1 tablespoon capers

1 tablespoon Dijon mustard

Dredge turkey in flour. Heat 1 tablespoon oil in a skillet over medium-high heat. Add cutlets and cook until golden brown, about 4 minutes per side. Remove turkey to a platter and cover.

Add remaining 1 tablespoon oil to the same skillet, add garlic and cook for 1 minute. Blend cornstarch with wine and add to the skillet with broth, capers and mustard. Bring to a boil and cook for 2 minutes, stirring frequently. Spoon sauce over turkey and serve immediately.

Serves 4

Turkey Tidbits

3 pounds boneless turkey breast, skinned and cut into 1 1/4-inch cubes

3 tablespoons dry sherry

1/2 cup peanut oil

1 tablespoon ground ginger

1 teaspoon lemon peel

4 green onions, sliced

3 tablespoons brown sugar

2/3 cup soy sauce

1 clove garlic, minced

1 teaspoon crushed red pepper

Place turkey in a covered container or ziplock bag. Combine remaining ingredients and pour over turkey. Refrigerate for 4 to 24 hours, turning occasionally.

Remove turkey from marinade and thread 1 inch apart on skewers. Grill over medium coals for 4 minutes per side or until done.

Serves 6

These tidbits also make great appetizers!

MEATS

Company's Coming Beef Rolls
160

Tenderloin Deluxe
161

Bleu Cheese Filets
with Brandy Sauce
161

Fantastic Filets
162

Herbed Tenderloin Steaks
with Mustard Sauce
163

Killer Flank Steak
163

Persian Skewers
164

Two Pepper Steak
165

Mexican Shredded Beef
166

Robin's Chunky Chili
167

Brandied Beef Stew
168

Crock Pot Beef Stroganoff
169

Walla Walla Steak Sandwich
with Horseradish Sauce
170

Best Focaccia Beef Sandwich
171

New Zealand BBQ Leg of Lamb
171

Cider Glazed Ham
with Golden Delicious Apples
172

Raspberry Grilled Pork
Tenderloin with Salad
173

Cranberry Pork Tenderloin
174

Marinated Pork Tenderloin
175

Washington Pork Chops
176

Huckleberry Pork Chops
177

Oriental Glazed Spareribs
177

Photo: Company's Coming Beef Rolls and New Potatoes with Herbed Shallot Butter

Company's Coming Beef Rolls

1/2 teaspoon garlic salt

2 tablespoons fresh parsley, chopped

1 (2-pound) flank steak, pounded

5 strips bacon, cooked until almost done but not crisp

kitchen string

Quick Hollandaise Sauce

3 egg yolks

2 tablespoons lemon juice

1/2 cup butter, melted

Never Fail Hollandaise Sauce

1/2 cup butter

1 1/2 tablespoons lemon juice

3 egg yolks

3 tablespoons boiling water

1/4 teaspoon salt

pinch cayenne pepper

Sprinkle garlic salt and parsley over top of steak. Arrange bacon strips on top of steak and roll lengthwise in a jelly-roll fashion. Secure rolled steak with kitchen string. (Steak may be prepared ahead to this point and refrigerated.) Cut steak into 2-inch rolls. Grill, cut side down, over medium coals for 10 minutes. Turn beef rolls and grill an additional 10 minutes or until cooked to desired doneness. Place beef rolls on plates and top with either hollandaise sauce.

For Quick Hollandaise Sauce, place egg yolks and lemon juice in a blender. Cover and quickly turn on and off. Turn blender to high and slowly drizzle melted butter into blender. Blend 30 seconds. Serve immediately.

For Never Fail Hollandaise Sauce, melt butter slowly in a small saucepan over low heat and keep warm. Place lemon juice in another small saucepan and heat until barely warm. Place egg yolks in the top of a double boiler filled with boiling water and beat with a wire whisk until thick. Whisk 1 tablespoon of boiling water into yolks. Repeat process with remaining 2 tablespoons of water. Beat in warm lemon juice and remove from double boiler. Beat sauce well with a wire whisk. Continue beating and gradually add the melted butter, salt and cayenne. Serve immediately.

Serves 4 to 6.

An easy yet elegant entree for an occasional splurge.

Tenderloin Deluxe

1 (2-pound) beef tenderloin

1 teaspoon butter

1/4 cup green onions, chopped

3/4 cup dry sherry

2 tablespoons soy sauce

1 teaspoon Dijon mustard

1 teaspoon black pepper

Place meat on a rack in a roasting pan and roast at 400° for 30 minutes. Meanwhile, melt butter in a small skillet over medium heat. Add onions and sauté until softened, about 4 minutes. Stir in sherry, soy sauce, mustard and pepper, heat through and set aside.

Pour sauce over meat after first 30 minutes of cooking time. Return tenderloin to oven and roast an additional 30 minutes, basting frequently. Check for desired doneness with a meat thermometer, 140° for rare, 160° for medium, 170° for well done. Serve with remaining sauce.

Serves 4

Bleu Cheese Filets with Brandy Sauce

1 tablespoon butter

2 (6-ounce) filet mignon steaks, cut 1 inch thick

1/2 teaspoon salt

1/4 teaspoon black pepper

2/3 cup beef broth

1/4 cup brandy

1 teaspoon fresh rosemary, chopped, or 1/2 teaspoon dried, crushed

1/2 cup bleu cheese, crumbled

Melt butter in a heavy skillet over medium-high heat. Season steaks with salt and pepper. Add steaks to skillet and sauté until cooked to desired doneness, about 4 minutes per side for medium rare. Transfer steaks to a plate and keep warm.

Add broth, brandy and rosemary to skillet, bring to a boil and cook until sauce is reduced to 1/3 cup, about 5 minutes. Spoon sauce over steaks. Top each steak with bleu cheese and serve immediately.

Serves 2

Fantastic Filets

1 teaspoon garlic, crushed and divided

1/2 tablespoon salt

1/4 teaspoon black pepper

8 (6 to 8-ounce) filet mignon steaks, cut 1 inch thick

5 tablespoons butter, divided

2 tablespoons brandy

3 tablespoons all-purpose flour

2 teaspoons tomato paste

3/4 cup dry red wine

1 cup chicken broth

1/2 cup beef broth

1/2 cup water

1/4 teaspoon Worcestershire sauce

2 tablespoons currant jelly

8 ounces mushrooms, sliced

Combine 1/2 teaspoon garlic, salt and pepper to make a paste. Rub paste on both sides of steaks. Heat 1 tablespoon butter in a large, heavy skillet (not non-stick) until it is very hot. Reduce heat to medium-high and sauté 3 steaks at a time until brown, about 2 minutes per side. If butter begins to burn, reduce heat slightly. Place steaks in baking pan(s) with at least 1-inch sides, leaving at least 1 inch between the steaks. Set aside.

De-glaze skillet with brandy over medium heat, stirring constantly to scrape up all the brown bits stuck to the bottom of the pan. Add remaining 4 tablespoons of butter, heat until melted and foamy, then stir in flour. Reduce heat to low and cook, stirring constantly, until mixture is golden. Stir in tomato paste and remaining 1/2 teaspoon garlic (the mixture will be thick and grainy). Remove pan from heat and whisk in wine, chicken broth, beef broth and water.

Return pan to stove and bring to a boil over medium heat, stirring constantly. Reduce heat and simmer, uncovered, for 10 minutes or until reduced by one-third, stirring occasionally. Stir in Worcestershire and jelly. When jelly has melted, stir in mushrooms and adjust seasonings if necessary. (Sauce should be of a coating consistency. Thin with water, broth or wine if necessary.)

When sauce has completely cooled, pour over steaks making sure that it does not come more than halfway up the steaks. (May be covered and refrigerated overnight at this point. If refrigerated, return to room temperature before cooking.)

Bake filets, uncovered, at 400° for 15 to 20 minutes (medium-rare) or 20 to 25 minutes (medium-well). (If baking in single oven on different racks, rotate halfway through baking time.) To serve, spoon sauce over steaks. Serve with additional sauce.

Serves 8

Herbed Tenderloin Steaks with Mustard Sauce

2 teaspoons dried thyme leaves, crumbled

1/2 teaspoon black pepper

4 (8-ounce) beef tenderloin steaks, 1 inch thick

1/2 cup beef broth

1/2 cup water

1/4 cup dry white wine

1 tablespoon butter

4 teaspoons Dijon mustard

2 tablespoons capers

Press thyme leaves and pepper into both sides of the beef. Heat a large non-stick skillet over medium-high heat for 2 minutes. Add steaks and cook 3 to 4 minutes on each side or to desired doneness. Remove to a platter and keep warm.

De-glaze the pan by adding broth, water and wine. Stir over high heat until the meat juices attached to the pan are dissolved and liquid is reduced to 2/3 cup. Whisk in butter and mustard until smooth. Reduce heat and stir in capers. Spoon sauce over steaks and serve.

Serves 4

Killer Flank Steak

1 (2-pound) flank steak, trimmed of fat

1/4 cup soy sauce

1/4 cup olive oil

1/2 tablespoon dried Italian seasoning

1 tablespoon lemon juice

2 cloves garlic, minced

Place steak in a covered container or ziplock bag. Combine remaining ingredients and pour over steak. Marinate at least 20 minutes at room temperature or up to 24 hours in the refrigerator, turning occasionally.

Grill over medium coals for 6 minutes. Turn and grill for an additional 6 to 8 minutes or until cooked to desired doneness. Slice thinly on the diagonal.

Serves 4

This is a deliciously different soy-based marinade!

Persian Skewers

Marinade

- 2 **tablespoons lemon juice**
- 1 **(8-ounce) container non-fat plain yogurt**
- 1/2 **cup onion, finely chopped**
- 1/4 **teaspoon ground oregano**
- 2 **cloves garlic, minced**
- 1/2 **teaspoon salt**
- 1/4 **teaspoon black pepper**

Skewers

- 2 **pounds sirloin steak, trimmed of fat and cut into 2-inch cubes**
- 2 **green peppers, cut into bite-sized pieces**
- 12 **mushrooms**
- 2 **medium onions, quartered**
- 1 **basket cherry tomatoes, stems removed**

Combine marinade ingredients in a shallow dish or ziplock bag. Add meat and refrigerate for 2 to 24 hours, turning occasionally.

When ready to cook, thread beef and vegetables on skewers. Grill over medium coals or broil in the oven, turning frequently, about 5 minutes per side, or until cooked to desired doneness.

Serves 6 to 8

Spray skewers with vegetable cooking spray before threading meat and vegetables to prevent sticking and ease in clean-up.

MEATS

Two Pepper Steak

1½ **pounds flank steak**

1½ **tablespoons Chinese rice wine**

4½ **tablespoons soy sauce**

1½ **teaspoons sugar**

1 **tablespoon cornstarch**

1 **tablespoon oil**

1 **large green pepper, cut into julienne strips**

1 **large red pepper, cut into julienne strips**

1 **(15-ounce) can baby corn on the cob**

5 **slices fresh ginger, peeled and cut ⅛-inch thick**

1 **cup rice, cooked**

Slice steak thinly across the grain into bite-sized strips. Mix wine, soy sauce, sugar and cornstarch together. Pour into covered container or ziplock bag and add steak slices, turning to coat thoroughly. (The steak can be cooked at once or marinated in the refrigerator for up to 6 hours.)

Heat oil in a wok or large skillet over high heat for about 30 seconds. Reduce heat to medium-high if oil begins to smoke. Immediately add peppers and corn and stir-fry until tender-crisp, about 3 minutes. Scoop out with a slotted spoon and reserve.

Add ginger to pan, stir-fry for a few seconds and then add steak with marinade. Stir-fry until meat is no longer pink, about 2 to 4 minutes. Discard the ginger. Return peppers and corn to the pan. Stir-fry until heated, about 1 minute. Transfer to heated platter and serve with cooked rice.

Serves 4

Mexican Shredded Beef

Filling

2 **pounds beef stew meat**

2¹/2 **cups water**

2 **cloves garlic, minced**

2 **tablespoons chili powder**

1 **tablespoon red wine vinegar**

2 **teaspoons dried oregano**

1 **teaspoon ground cumin**

1 **teaspoon salt**

¹/8 **teaspoon black pepper**

Tortillas

12 **(10-inch) flour tortillas, stacked**

Condiments

shredded lettuce

guacamole

sour cream

salsa

Combine filling ingredients in a Dutch oven. Bring to a boil, cover, reduce heat and simmer for 2 hours or until the meat is very tender. Uncover and boil rapidly for about 15 minutes or until liquid has almost evaporated. Stir frequently during the final cooking time to prevent meat from sticking to pan. Remove meat from pan and shred, using two forks.

Wrap tortillas in foil and heat in the oven at 350° for about 15 minutes. Spoon about 1/4 cup beef filling in each tortilla and roll up. Serve with condiments.

Serves 8 to 10

This filling can be prepared up to one day ahead of time, making this an easy last minute meal.

Robin's Chunky Chili

1 pound spicy Italian link sausage, diagonally cut into 1-inch chunks

1 pound ground beef

1 medium red onion, cut into 3/4-inch chunks

1 green pepper, cut into 3/4-inch chunks

2 cloves garlic, crushed

1 1/2 cups dry red wine

3/4 cup Worcestershire sauce

3 tablespoons chili powder

1 tablespoon black pepper

1 1/2 teaspoons celery seed

1 teaspoon dry mustard

3 (16-ounce) cans whole tomatoes, with liquid

1 (12-ounce) can tomato paste

1 (25-ounce) can red kidney beans, with liquid

hot pepper sauce, optional

Garnishes

shredded cheddar cheese

sour cream

sliced green onions

sliced black olives

Brown sausage in a large saucepan, drain and set aside. Add ground beef to pan and cook until brown. Drain and set aside. Add onion, green pepper and garlic and sauté until tender, about 5 minutes.

Stir in red wine and Worcestershire. Simmer, uncovered, for 10 minutes. Stir in chili powder, pepper, celery seed and mustard. Simmer, uncovered, over low heat for 10 minutes.

Return meats to the pan and add tomatoes and tomato paste. Bring mixture to a boil, cover and simmer for 30 minutes, stirring occasionally.

Add kidney beans and season with hot pepper sauce, if desired. Cover and simmer for one hour. (Can be refrigerated at this point and re-heated prior to serving.) Serve with desired garnishes.

Serves 12 to 16

It's not a misprint - this chili calls for 3/4 cup Worcestershire sauce, but don't let that scare you off...it's out of this world!

Brandied Beef Stew

2 pounds boneless beef bottom round, trimmed of fat and cut into 1-inch cubes

1/2 cup brandy

3 (12 1/2-ounce) cans low-fat beef broth, divided

1 cup (about 1 large) onion, finely chopped

1/2 cup shallots, thinly sliced

1/2 teaspoon salt

1/2 teaspoon black pepper

1/4 cup plus 1 tablespoon Dijon mustard, divided

3/4 cup (about 3 medium) carrots, cut into 1/2-inch slices

12 small new potatoes, halved

1/2 tablespoon butter

1/2 pound small mushrooms, quartered

1/4 cup dry red wine

Combine beef, brandy and 1/4 cup broth in a wide 4-quart pan. Cover and simmer over medium heat for 30 minutes.

Add onion, shallots, salt and pepper. Cook, uncovered, until most of the liquid has evaporated and juices and onion are browned, about 20 minutes, stirring occasionally. Add 1/4 cup mustard and remaining beef broth, stirring to loosen any browned bits. Cover, reduce heat and simmer until beef is almost tender when pierced, about 1 hour.

Stir in carrots and potatoes, cover and continue cooking until vegetables are tender, about 45 minutes.

Melt butter in a skillet over medium-high heat. Add mushrooms and wine and cook until most of the liquid has evaporated and mushrooms are soft, stirring often. Blend in remaining 1 tablespoon mustard. Stir mixture into stew and serve.

Serves 6

Beef and chicken broth can be made fat-free by placing the can in the refrigerator for one hour and removing fat after opening.

Crock Pot Beef Stroganoff

2 pounds round steak, cut into small strips

1 teaspoon salt

1/8 teaspoon black pepper

1 medium (about 1/2 cup) onion, sliced and rings separated

2 beef bouillon cubes, dissolved in 1 cup hot water

1/2 teaspoon garlic salt

1/4 teaspoon Worcestershire sauce

1 tablespoon catsup

1 tablespoon butter

1 cup (about 4 ounces) mushrooms, sliced

2 tablespoons dry white wine, optional

1/3 cup all-purpose flour

1/3 cup cold water

1 cup sour cream

cooked noodles or rice

Season steak with salt and pepper and place in the bottom of a crock pot. Top with onion rings. Combine bouillon, garlic salt, Worcestershire and catsup. Pour over meat. Cover and cook on low for 6 to 8 hours.

Melt butter in a skillet over medium heat, add mushrooms and sauté for about 5 minutes. Transfer mushrooms to crock pot and add wine, if desired. Dissolve flour in cold water and add to crock pot, stirring until well blended. Increase crock pot heat to high and cook for 15 minutes or until sauce is thickened. Stir in sour cream and serve over noodles or rice.

Serves 6

Dust off your crock pot and discover a do-ahead family favorite.

Walla Walla Steak Sandwich with Horseradish Sauce

2 **pounds flank steak**

Marinade

3/4 **cup beer**

1/4 **cup olive oil**

1 **teaspoon salt**

1/2 **teaspoon black pepper**

2 **cloves garlic, minced**

1/4 **teaspoon crushed red pepper**

Onions

3 **tablespoons butter**

3/4 **teaspoon paprika**

6 **cups Walla Walla sweet onions, sliced into 1/4-inch rings**

Horseradish Sauce

1 **cup sour cream**

2 **tablespoons horseradish**

1 **tablespoon parsley**

1/4 **teaspoon salt**

1/8 **teaspoon paprika**

Rolls

1/4 **cup butter, softened**

1 **tablespoon Italian herb seasoning**

6 **French rolls, split**

Trim steak of fat and score both sides. Place in a covered container or ziplock bag. Combine marinade ingredients and add to steak. Refrigerate for 4 to 24 hours, turning occasionally.

Melt butter in a large skillet over medium-low heat. Add paprika and onions and sauté until onions are tender, about 20 to 25 minutes. Keep warm until ready to serve.

Combine sauce ingredients in a small saucepan and cook over low heat until thoroughly heated, about 7 minutes. Keep warm until ready to serve.

Remove steak from marinade and grill or broil about 5 minutes per side or until steak reaches desired degree of doneness. Slice steak thinly on the diagonal and keep warm until ready to serve.

Combine butter and Italian seasoning and spread on rolls. Toast rolls briefly under broiler. To serve, place steak on rolls, top with onions and sauce.

Serves 6

If you can't find Walla Walla sweets, substitute Vidalia or Maui onions. Be sure to sauté them slowly over low heat to bring out their natural sweetness.

Best Focaccia Beef Sandwich

Marinade

- 1/4 **cup vegetable oil**
- 1/4 **cup olive oil**
- 1/2 **cup white wine vinegar**
- 2 **teaspoons Dijon mustard**
- 2 **teaspoons dried parsley**

Sandwich

- 1 **pound deli-style roast beef**
- 3 **avocados, sliced**
- 1 **small red onion, thinly sliced**
- 1 **loaf focaccia bread**
- **olive oil**

Combine marinade ingredients and place in a covered pan or ziplock bag. Add beef, avocados and onion. Refrigerate overnight.

When ready to assemble sandwich, brush focaccia lightly with oil and bake at 375° for 12 to 15 minutes or until lightly browned. Slice focaccia horizontally in half. Remove beef, avocados and onions from marinade and arrange on top of the bottom half of focaccia. Top with other half of focaccia. Slice into wedges and serve.

Serves 6 to 8

Adding monterey jack cheese to this sandwich is an enjoyable option.

New Zealand BBQ Leg of Lamb

- 1 **boneless short cut leg of lamb (5 to 6 pounds), butterflied**
- 1 **orange, zested and juiced**
- 1 **teaspoon red currant jelly**
- 2 **tablespoons white wine**
- 1 **tablespoon Dijon mustard**
- 1 **clove garlic, crushed**
- 1 **tablespoon vegetable oil**

Place lamb in a covered pan or ziplock bag. Combine remaining ingredients and add to lamb. Refrigerate for 6 to 8 hours, turning occasionally.

Remove lamb from marinade and grill for 15 minutes, turn and cook an additional 15 minutes or until cooked through, being careful not to burn meat. Baste with marinade while cooking.

Serves 8

Cider Glazed Ham with Golden Delicious Apples

1 (10-pound) cook-before-
    you-eat ham

3 cups non-alcoholic sparkling
    cider, divided

Glaze

1 tablespoon Dijon mustard

1 cup brown sugar

20 cloves

Apples

8 to 10 (about 4 pounds) small
    Golden Delicious apples

½ cup golden raisins

½ cup brown sugar

Sauce

¼ cup brandy

3 tablespoons golden raisins

½ teaspoon nutmeg

½ teaspoon ground cloves

Place ham in a roasting pan and pour half of the cider over it. Bake at 350° until internal temperature reaches 170°, about 3 to 3 1/2 hours. While baking, pour additional cider over ham every 30 minutes to keep it moist. Remove ham from oven, let cool slightly and carefully carve visible fat from the ham.

Combine mustard and sugar in a bowl to make the glaze. Spread mixture over the ham. Push cloves into meat at even intervals. Return ham to roasting pan.

Score each apple in a horizontal circle with a knife to prevent bursting during baking. Combine raisins and sugar. Remove the core from each apple with an apple corer or vegetable peeler. Cut a slice from the end of each core and replace it in the bottom of each apple. Stuff raisin mixture into other end of the apple. Arrange apples in the roasting pan around the ham.

Increase oven temperature to 400° and continue baking the ham until the surface has a shiny glaze, about 30 minutes. Baste ham with pan juices every 10 minutes, adding more cider if necessary. Transfer ham to board or serving platter and carve.

Pour drippings into a saucepan and skim off as much grease as possible. Pour brandy into the juices and whisk while bringing to a boil. If the sauce is too thick, add more apple cider. Add raisins and simmer for about 2 minutes. Whisk in nutmeg and ground cloves. Heat sauce through and transfer to a sauce boat for serving.

Serves 8 to 10

Raspberry Grilled Pork Tenderloin with Salad

2 (12-ounce) pork tenderloins

Marinade

1/2 cup raspberry vinegar

2 cloves garlic, minced

1 tablespoon honey

1 tablespoon Dijon mustard

1/2 teaspoon dried marjoram

1/2 teaspoon dried thyme

1/2 teaspoon black pepper

Salad

6 tablespoons olive oil

10 cups salad greens, rinsed and torn

1/4 teaspoon salt or to taste

Place pork in a covered container or ziplock bag. Combine marinade ingredients and mix well. Pour 1/2 cup marinade over tenderloins. Refrigerate for 2 to 24 hours, turning occasionally.

Add oil to remaining marinade and mix well to prepare dressing for greens. Cover and set aside until ready to serve, refrigerating if overnight.

Remove pork from marinade and grill over medium coals, turning to brown on all sides, until a meat thermometer reaches 150°, about 15 minutes. Baste tenderloins with marinade as they cook. Slice into medallions.

Toss desired amount of dressing with salad greens and serve as an accompaniment to the pork, adding salt to taste.

Serves 4 to 6

A main dish and side salad all in one - include some garlic rolls and dinner is served!

Cranberry Pork Tenderloin

3 cloves garlic, minced

2 teaspoons black pepper, divided

2 tablespoons fresh thyme, chopped, or 2 teaspoons dried, divided

3 pounds pork tenderloin

1 fifth (about 3 cups) ruby or tawny port wine

1 cup whipping cream

2 tablespoons shallots, minced

1/2 cup dried cranberries

Combine garlic, 1 teaspoon pepper and 1 tablespoon fresh or 1 teaspoon dried thyme. Rub mixture on tenderloins, cover and refrigerate for 6 hours or overnight.

When ready to cook, prepare sauce by pouring port into a medium saucepan. Bring to a boil and cook until reduced to 1 cup, about 25 minutes. Add cream, shallots, remaining 1 teaspoon pepper and remaining thyme. Cook over low heat until sauce starts to thicken. Add cranberries and heat thoroughly. (Can be made up to 24 hours in advance and refrigerated. Re-heat gently.)

Broil or grill pork over medium coals for about 15 minutes, turning so that all sides are brown. Slice and serve with port sauce.

Serves 8 to 10

Marinated Pork Tenderloin

3 pounds pork tenderloin

Marinade

8 Brazil nuts, shelled

2 tablespoons ground coriander

1/4 teaspoon black pepper

1/8 teaspoon cayenne pepper

1 clove garlic, minced

1 tablespoon brown sugar

3 tablespoons lemon juice

1 teaspoon salt

1/4 cup soy sauce

1/4 cup olive oil

2 tablespoons onion,
   finely chopped

Place pork in a covered container or ziplock bag. Combine marinade ingredients in a food processor or blender and process until nuts are chopped. Add marinade to pork. Refrigerate for 2 to 24 hours, turning occasionally.

Just before cooking, remove pork from marinade. Broil or grill over medium coals, turning to brown all sides, about 15 minutes. Slice into medallions and serve.

Serves 6

Pork cooked to an internal temperature of 150° will have a tinge of pink and be juicy.

Washington Pork Chops

1½ tablespoons butter, divided

2 cups apple, peeled, cored and chopped

1 teaspoon honey

1 teaspoon lemon juice

¼ cup all-purpose flour

½ teaspoon salt

¼ teaspoon black pepper

4 boneless pork chops (about 1-inch thick)

1 cup chicken broth

1 cup apple juice

½ cup cranberry juice

¼ cup brandy

1 (1-inch piece) cinnamon stick

fresh chives, chopped for garnish

Melt 1/2 tablespoon butter in a skillet over medium heat. Add apple, honey and lemon juice. Sauté until apple is tender and golden, about 4 minutes. Set aside and keep warm.

Place flour, salt and pepper in a bowl. Dredge chops in flour mixture. Melt remaining 1 tablespoon butter in another skillet. Add pork chops and cook for 5 to 6 minutes. Turn chops over and cook for an additional 5 minutes or until no longer pink and thoroughly cooked. Transfer to a warm platter and cover.

Add broth, apple and cranberry juices, brandy and cinnamon to the skillet and bring to a boil, scraping up browned bits. Simmer, uncovered, until reduced to 2/3 cup, about 15 minutes. Discard cinnamon stick and stir in apples. Return chops to skillet and warm through. Place chops on plates, top with apple mixture, sprinkle with chives and serve immediately.

Serves 4

Especially good with Golden Delicious apples!

Huckleberry Pork Chops

vegetable cooking spray

6 center-cut loin pork chops
(about 2 pounds total),
trimmed of fat

freshly ground black pepper

3 tablespoons huckleberry jam
or black currant preserves

1½ tablespoons Dijon mustard

¼ cup raspberry or
white wine vinegar

Coat a large frying pan with cooking spray and place over medium-high heat. Sprinkle pork chops generously with pepper, add to pan and brown on both sides, turning once, about 8 to 10 minutes total.

Combine jam and mustard and spoon over chops. Reduce heat to medium-low, cover and cook an additional 6 to 8 minutes or until chops are thoroughly cooked but still moist and slightly pink in center. Remove chops to a platter and keep warm.

Add vinegar to pan, increase heat to medium-high and stir to loosen any browned bits. Bring sauce to a boil and cook, uncovered, until reduced to 1/4 cup, about 2 to 3 minutes. Spoon sauce over chops and serve immediately.

Serves 6

Oriental Glazed Spareribs

4 to 5 pounds pork spareribs

Marinade

1 cup soy sauce

1 cup orange marmalade

3 cloves garlic, finely chopped

1 teaspoon ground ginger

⅛ teaspoon black pepper

Place spareribs in a covered container or ziplock bag. Combine marinade ingredients and mix well. Pour marinade over ribs. Refrigerate overnight, turning occasionally to coat ribs.

Remove ribs from marinade, reserving marinade, and arrange on a rack in a roasting pan. Bake at 350° for 1 hour and 30 minutes. Baste with remaining marinade every 15 to 20 minutes until ribs are glazed and browned and meat is tender.

Serves 6

VEGETABLES & SIDE DISHES

Wild Rice and Cranberry Pilaf
180

Washington Wild Rice
180

Curried Pilaf with Corn
181

Paradise Rice with Bean Sprouts
181

Mexican Black Beans with Rice
182

Rice Pilaf with Mushrooms and Pecans
182

Pilaf-Style Couscous
183

Orzo with Parmesan and Pesto
183

Garlic Mashed Potatoes
184

Smashing Potatoes
184

New Potatoes with Herbed Shallot Butter
185

New Potatoes and Leeks Dijon
185

Celebration Potato Puffs
186

Light & Fluffy Sweet Potato Soufflé
187

Herbed Potatoes in Parchment
188

Sautéed Artichoke Hearts
with Red Bell Peppers
188

Sautéed Mushrooms with Sherry
189

One at a Thyme Spinach Soufflés
190

Italian Spinach Sauté
191

Marinated Asparagus
191

Asparagus Pignolias
192

Orange-Glazed Asparagus
192

Zucchini & Feta Fantastic
193

One Hundred and One Zucchini
193

Herb Roasted Vegetables
194

Vegetable Pie
195

Carrots for Kids
196

Mustard Dill Baby Carrots
196

Sensational Cauliflower
197

Colorful Corn Sauté
198

Herbed Green Beans with Pine Nuts
199

A Bundle of Beans
199

Fabulous Four Pepper Stir-Fry
200

Spicy Summer Cucumbers
201

Photo: Fabulous Four Pepper Stir-Fry

Wild Rice and Cranberry Pilaf

3/4 cup wild rice, uncooked
and rinsed

3 cups chicken broth

1/2 cup pearl barley

1/4 cup dried cranberries or
cherries, chopped

1/4 cup currants

1 tablespoon butter

1/3 cup sliced almonds, toasted

Combine rice and broth in a saucepan and bring to a boil. Reduce heat, cover and simmer for 10 minutes.

Combine barley, cranberries, currants and butter in a casserole dish. Add rice mixture and stir well. Cover and bake at 350° for 50 to 60 minutes, stirring once. Wild rice is done when it is tender and the liquid is absorbed.

Fluff rice mixture with a fork and stir in toasted almonds.

Serves 6

Washington Wild Rice

1/4 cup butter

1 cup wild rice, uncooked
and rinsed

8 ounces wild or cultivated
mushrooms, sliced

2 (14 1/2-ounce) cans
chicken broth

Melt butter in a large skillet over medium heat. Add rice and mushrooms and sauté for 10 minutes. Transfer rice mixture to a casserole dish. Pour in broth, cover and bake at 325° until the liquid is absorbed, about 2 hours. Serve immediately or cool, refrigerate and re-heat prior to serving.

Serves 6

Curried Pilaf with Corn

1 tablespoon vegetable oil

1/2 teaspoon cumin seeds

1 cup long grain rice, uncooked

2 tablespoons fresh chives

3/4 teaspoon curry powder

1/4 teaspoon salt

1/4 teaspoon black pepper

1 1/4 cups frozen corn, thawed

1/3 cup water

1 (14 1/2-ounce) can low-fat chicken broth

2 tablespoons dry roasted peanuts, chopped

Heat oil in a large saucepan over medium heat. Add cumin seeds and sauté for 1 minute. Add rice, chives, curry, salt, pepper and corn and cook for 1 minute, stirring constantly. Add water and broth and bring to a boil. Reduce heat and cover. Simmer until liquid is absorbed, about 20 minutes.

Remove saucepan from heat and let stand, covered, for 5 minutes. Stir in peanuts and serve immediately.

Serves 4 to 6

Even if you aren't a fan of curry you'll love this versatile dish!

Paradise Rice with Bean Sprouts

2 tablespoons butter

2/3 cup long grain rice, uncooked

1/4 pound fresh bean sprouts, rinsed and drained

1/4 cup green onions, thinly sliced

1 1/3 cups chicken broth

1/3 cup macadamia nuts, chopped

Melt butter in a large skillet over medium heat. Add rice and sauté until golden brown, about 4 to 5 minutes. Add bean sprouts and onions. Sauté until onions are soft, about 2 minutes.

Stir in broth and bring to a boil. Cover, reduce heat and simmer 20 minutes or until the liquid has been absorbed. Toss with macadamia nuts just prior to serving.

Serves 4 to 6

Mexican Black Beans with Rice

2 (16-ounce) cans black beans

1 (15-ounce) can Mexican-style stewed tomatoes

1 (4½-ounce) can chopped green chilies

¼ cup barbecue sauce

½ teaspoon ground cumin

1 tablespoon lime juice

1 cup frozen corn kernels

1 cup rice, cooked

Drain and rinse beans. Combine beans, tomatoes, chilies, barbecue sauce, cumin and lime juice in a medium saucepan. Bring to a boil and simmer, uncovered, for 5 minutes. Add corn and simmer an additional 5 minutes.

Spoon beans over rice.

Serves 6

You don't have to be a vegetarian to love this easy dish. It's also delicious rolled in a tortilla.

Rice Pilaf with Mushrooms and Pecans

vegetable cooking spray

2 cups mushrooms, sliced

½ cup green onions, sliced

1 (10½-ounce) can beef consommé

1¼ cups water

1 cup long grain white rice, uncooked

¼ cup pecans, chopped and toasted

⅛ teaspoon black pepper

Coat a saucepan with cooking spray. Add mushrooms and onions. Sauté over medium-high heat for 5 minutes or until mushrooms and onions are soft. Stir in consommé, water and rice and bring to a boil. Cover, reduce heat and simmer until rice is tender and liquid is absorbed, about 20 minutes.

Stir in pecans and pepper just before serving.

Serves 4

Pilaf-Style Couscous

1 tablespoon olive oil

1/2 cup green onions, sliced

1/2 cup celery, finely chopped

3 tablespoons currants

2 tablespoons pine nuts

1 cup couscous

1 1/2 cups chicken broth

1/2 teaspoon salt

1/4 teaspoon black pepper

Heat oil in a heavy saucepan. Add onions, celery, currants and pine nuts. Sauté over medium heat for 3 minutes or until onions are soft. Stir in couscous and cook until lightly toasted, about 1 minute.

Add broth, salt and pepper. Bring mixture to a boil, stirring gently. Cover the pan, remove from heat and let couscous stand for 5 minutes. Just before serving, fluff with a fork.

Serves 4

Orzo with Parmesan and Pesto

3 tablespoons butter

1 1/2 cups orzo

3 cups chicken broth

1/2 cup Parmesan cheese, grated

2 tablespoons basil pesto

fresh basil sprigs, optional

Melt butter in a skillet over medium-high heat. Add orzo and sauté for 2 minutes. Add broth and bring to a boil. Cover and reduce heat. Simmer until orzo is tender and liquid is absorbed, about 20 minutes. Stir in Parmesan and pesto. Transfer to a serving bowl and garnish with fresh basil sprigs, if desired.

Serves 6

Garlic Mashed Potatoes

3 **pounds white potatoes (about 7 cups), peeled and cut into 1-inch cubes**

1 **large (1½-ounce) head garlic**

¼ **cup whipping cream**

¼ **cup butter, softened**

¼ **cup Parmesan cheese, freshly grated**

1 **teaspoon salt**

½ **teaspoon freshly ground black pepper**

Place potatoes in a large saucepan, cover with cold water and bring to a boil. Reduce heat slightly and cook until tender, about 20 minutes. Drain potatoes and return to hot saucepan. Shake over medium heat to remove remaining moisture, about 15 seconds. Set aside.

Meanwhile, peel garlic and separate cloves. Place cloves in a small saucepan and cover with water. Bring to a boil, lower heat and simmer until garlic is soft, about 15 minutes. Drain and cool.

Remove skin from cooked garlic, place garlic in a processor, add the cream and purée. Mash potatoes with an electric mixer. Add puréed garlic mixture, butter, Parmesan, salt and pepper and beat until smooth. Serve immediately. Re-heat in microwave if necessary.

Serves 6 to 8

Smashing Potatoes

5 **pounds white potatoes, peeled**

6 **ounces cream cheese, softened**

1 **cup sour cream**

2 **teaspoons garlic salt**

1 **teaspoon salt**

¼ **teaspoon black pepper**

3 **tablespoons butter**

Cook potatoes in boiling water until tender. Drain and mash until smooth. Beat in remaining ingredients until light and fluffy. Cool, cover and refrigerate overnight or up to 7 days.

Place potatoes in a greased casserole, dot with additional butter, if desired, and bake at 350° for 30 minutes or until thoroughly heated.

Serves 12

New Potatoes with Herbed Shallot Butter

1 1/4 pounds small new potatoes

1 tablespoon butter

1/3 cup shallots, finely chopped

2 cloves garlic, minced

1/2 teaspoon dried tarragon

1/2 teaspoon dried chives

1 teaspoon fresh parsley, chopped, or 1/2 teaspoon dried

1/4 teaspoon salt

1/8 teaspoon black pepper

Cook potatoes in boiling water until just tender, about 15 minutes. Drain and keep warm.

Melt butter in a large skillet. Add shallots and garlic and sauté over low heat until softened, about 5 minutes.

Add cooked potatoes and stir well. Stir in remaining ingredients and cook until potatoes are thoroughly heated.

Serves 6

Choose plump and well shaped shallots. Avoid those which appear dry or have sprouted.

New Potatoes and Leeks Dijon

vegetable cooking spray

1/2 cup leeks, cut into 1/4-inch slices

1 1/2 pounds small new potatoes, cut into quarters

1 cup chicken broth

1/2 cup dry white wine

1 tablespoon Dijon mustard

1/4 teaspoon black pepper

Coat a small skillet with cooking spray and heat to medium. Add leeks and sauté until tender, about 3 to 5 minutes.

Combine potatoes, broth, wine and mustard in a medium saucepan. Bring to a boil, reduce heat, cover and simmer for 6 minutes. Uncover and simmer until potatoes are tender, about 15 minutes. Add leeks to potatoes and cook until mixture is thoroughly heated. Season with pepper.

Serves 4

Celebration Potato Puffs

2 pounds white potatoes, peeled

3 ounces cream cheese, softened

1/4 cup milk

1/4 cup Parmesan cheese, grated

1 tablespoon green onions, sliced

1/2 tablespoon butter, melted

2 1/2 teaspoons instant onion soup mix

1/2 teaspoon seasoned salt

1/2 teaspoon black pepper

dash hot pepper sauce

1 large egg, beaten

1 1/2 cups cornflake crumbs

Cook, drain and mash the potatoes. Beat in the remaining ingredients except the egg and cornflake crumbs. Using an ice cream scoop, form mashed potatoes into balls. (Chilling potatoes for at least one hour makes them easier to handle.)

Dip balls in beaten egg and roll in cornflake crumbs. Place on a greased cookie sheet. (May be prepared ahead to this point. Cover and refrigerate.)

Bake at 400° until thoroughly heated, about 10 minutes, 30 minutes if refrigerated.

Serves 6 to 8

Light & Fluffy Sweet Potato Soufflé

5 cups (about 2 pounds) sweet
potatoes, peeled and cubed, or
5 cups canned sweet potatoes,
drained and cubed

1 cup unsweetened applesauce

1 egg yolk

1 teaspoon vanilla extract

½ teaspoon cinnamon

2 egg whites

vegetable cooking spray

½ cup brown sugar

2 tablespoons all-purpose flour

1 tablespoon margarine, melted

Cook fresh potatoes in boiling water for 15 minutes or until tender, drain and cool.

Combine potatoes and applesauce in a processor or mixer until smooth. Add egg yolk, vanilla and cinnamon. Mix until smooth. Set aside.

Beat egg whites until stiff peaks form. Gently fold egg whites into potato mixture and spoon into a 1 1/2-quart soufflé dish that has been coated with cooking spray. (May be made up to 24 hours ahead. Cover and refrigerate.)

Combine sugar, flour and margarine. Sprinkle over potato mixture and bake at 350° for 35 to 45 minutes or until set.

Serves 8 to 10

Try this for your next holiday buffet.

Herbed Potatoes in Parchment

1½ pounds small red or white new
    potatoes, scrubbed

2 teaspoons olive oil

1 tablespoon dried parsley

1 teaspoon dried thyme

1 teaspoon dried sage

½ teaspoon salt

    parchment or aluminum foil

Halve any potatoes that are significantly larger than the others. Combine oil, herbs and salt and pour over potatoes. Toss to coat.

Cut a sheet of parchment paper approximately 18 x 36-inches. Transfer potatoes to one half of paper. Fold paper loosely over potatoes and seal by crimping edges together. Place on baking sheet and bake at 350° for 60 minutes.

Serves 6

Sautéed Artichoke Hearts with Red Bell Peppers

2 teaspoons olive oil

2 large cloves garlic, chopped

1 (14-ounce) can artichoke
    hearts, drained and quartered

2 red bell peppers, cut into
    1-inch chunks

1½ tablespoons balsamic vinegar

¼ cup green onions, sliced

⅛ teaspoon dried thyme

½ teaspoon dried basil

¼ teaspoon black pepper

Heat oil in a large skillet over medium heat. Add garlic and sauté for 1 minute. Add artichoke hearts and bell peppers. Cook gently until just tender, about 3 to 5 minutes. Add remaining ingredients and heat thoroughly. Serve immediately.

Serves 4 to 6

Sautéed Mushrooms with Sherry

vegetable cooking spray

1 teaspoon oil

4 cups (about 1 pound) medium mushrooms, cleaned, stemmed and quartered

1/4 cup green onions, chopped

1 clove garlic, sliced

1/2 cup sherry

3/4 cup tomatoes (about 2 medium), seeded and chopped

1/2 teaspoon dried thyme

1/4 teaspoon salt

1/8 teaspoon black pepper

1 teaspoon cornstarch, dissolved in 1 tablespoon water

1 tablespoon fresh parsley, chopped

Coat a heavy skillet with cooking spray, add oil and heat to medium-high. Add mushrooms and sauté for 1 minute. Add onions and garlic and sauté for 1 more minute.

Stir in sherry, tomatoes, thyme, salt and pepper. Cook, uncovered, until the mushrooms have softened, about 3 to 4 minutes. Stir in the cornstarch mixture, and cook until the liquid is slightly thickened, about 2 minutes.

Transfer mushroom mixture to a serving dish and sprinkle with chopped parsley. (May be prepared a few hours in advance. Cover and refrigerate. Re-heat in the microwave.)

Serves 4

When you need a change of pace, serve this side dish with grilled meats or poultry.

One at a Thyme Spinach Soufflés

2 eggs

1 egg yolk

1½ cups milk

3 tablespoons Parmesan cheese

2 (10-ounce) packages frozen chopped spinach, thawed and well drained

1½ cups fresh bread crumbs

¼ teaspoon salt

⅛ teaspoon black pepper

Dressing

2 tablespoons lemon juice

1 teaspoon sugar

½ teaspoon Dijon mustard

½ teaspoon fresh thyme leaves, chopped, or ⅛ teaspoon dried

¼ cup olive oil

1 cup Roma tomatoes (about 4), seeded and diced

Beat whole eggs and egg yolk in a bowl. Heat milk just to boiling and beat into the eggs. Add Parmesan and then fold in the spinach, bread crumbs, salt and pepper.

Butter 6 ramekins or custard cups. Spoon spinach mixture into prepared ramekins and cover each tightly with foil. (Soufflés may be prepared, covered and refrigerated until ready to bake.)

Place covered ramekins in a shallow baking pan and add hot water to the pan so that it comes halfway up the sides of the ramekins. Bake at 350° for about 35 minutes (longer if refrigerated) or until a knife inserted in the soufflé comes out clean.

Prepare the dressing by combining the lemon juice, sugar, mustard, thyme and oil. Stir in tomatoes. Set aside.

To serve, unmold the soufflés onto individual plates and spoon a little dressing over each soufflé.

Serves 6

This show stopper adds color to any plate!

Italian Spinach Sauté

1/4 **cup olive oil**

3 **cloves garlic, crushed**

1 **bunch fresh spinach (about 6 ounces), washed, stems trimmed and well drained**

1/4 **cup water**

1/2 **teaspoon salt**

1/2 **teaspoon black pepper**

1/4 **cup sliced almonds**

Heat oil in a large skillet over medium heat. Add garlic and sauté until golden brown, about 3 minutes. Add spinach and water to skillet. Cover and let cook for 30 seconds. Stir spinach and remove from heat. Cover and let rest for 4 minutes. Drain. Season with salt and pepper and place in a serving bowl. Sprinkle with almonds and serve immediately.

Serves 4 to 6

Marinated Asparagus

1 **pound fresh asparagus, trimmed**

Marinade

1/2 **cup vegetable oil**

1/4 **cup lemon juice**

2 **tablespoons celery, chopped**

1 **teaspoon chives, minced**

2 **teaspoons salt**

1/2 **teaspoon freshly ground black pepper**

1/2 **teaspoon paprika**

Steam asparagus until tender-crisp, about 10 minutes. Plunge in cold water and drain well.

Combine marinade ingredients and pour over asparagus. Cover and refrigerate until ready to serve.

Serves 4

Marinated asparagus will keep in the refrigerator for up to one week.

Asparagus Pignolias

1 pound fresh asparagus, trimmed

3 tablespoons unsalted butter

1 teaspoon garlic, minced

1/4 cup prosciutto, chopped

1/2 teaspoon dried basil

3 tablespoons pine nuts, toasted

freshly ground black pepper

4 tablespoons Parmesan cheese, grated and divided

Cook asparagus in boiling water for 6 minutes or until tender-crisp. Drain and rinse immediately under cold water. Transfer to broiler-proof dish.

Melt butter in a small saucepan over medium heat. Add garlic and sauté for 2 minutes. Add prosciutto and sauté for an additional 2 minutes.

Combine basil, nuts, pepper and 2 tablespoons Parmesan. Add prosciutto mixture and combine well. Spread over asparagus and sprinkle with remaining 2 tablespoons Parmesan. Broil for 2 minutes or until cheese has almost melted.

Serves 4

Orange-Glazed Asparagus

2 pounds fresh asparagus

1/2 cup orange juice

1/2 teaspoon dried orange peel

1 tablespoon sugar

1 tablespoon fresh ginger, minced

2 teaspoons soy sauce

Trim asparagus and place in a covered container or ziplock bag. Combine remaining ingredients and pour over asparagus. Refrigerate for 2 to 24 hours, turning occasionally.

Drain asparagus and reserve marinade. Place asparagus on a baking sheet. Broil for 5 minutes or until tender, turning several times to prevent burning.

Meanwhile, place marinade in a small saucepan and bring to a boil. Continue to simmer, uncovered, until marinade is reduced by half. Transfer cooked asparagus to serving dish and top with marinade.

Serves 6

Zucchini & Feta Fantastic

1 cup zucchini (about 1 small), cut into 1/4-inch slices

1 cup green pepper (about 1), cut into 1/4-inch strips

1/2 cup onion rings, separated

1/2 teaspoon dried oregano leaves, crushed

1 tablespoon butter

1/2 cup cherry tomatoes, halved

3/4 cup (4 ounces) feta cheese, crumbled

Combine zucchini, pepper, onion rings, oregano and butter in a microwave dish. Cover, vent and cook on high for 4 minutes, stirring once. Add tomatoes and cook for 1 additional minute. Toss with cheese and serve immediately.

Serves 6

One Hundred and One Zucchini

3 cups zucchini, shredded

1 cup buttery cracker crumbs, crushed

1 cup sharp cheddar cheese, shredded

2 eggs, beaten

3 tablespoons onion, minced

1/4 teaspoon salt

1/8 teaspoon black pepper

1/2 cup tomato, chopped

Combine all ingredients except tomato and spread in a greased 8-inch square baking dish. Bake at 350° for 50 to 60 minutes. Garnish with chopped tomato and serve immediately. (May be prepared 6 to 8 hours ahead and refrigerated prior to baking.)

Serves 4 to 6

This is a great way to use up extra zucchini from your garden!

Herb Roasted Vegetables

1 red bell pepper, quartered, seeded, and cut into triangles

1 yellow bell pepper, quartered, seeded, and cut into triangles

2 medium-sized sweet onions, peeled and cut into 1-inch wedges

5 medium red potatoes, cut into 1-inch pieces

2 small zucchini squash, halved lengthwise and cut into 1-inch slices

2 small yellow squash, halved lengthwise and cut into 1-inch slices

Marinade

4 to 6 cloves garlic, minced

2 tablespoons olive oil

1 tablespoon balsamic vinegar

2 tablespoons each fresh rosemary, thyme and parsley, chopped, or 1 tablespoon each dried

Topping

1/2 cup Parmesan cheese, grated, optional

Place vegetables in a 9 x 13-inch roasting pan. Combine marinade ingredients and toss with vegetables. Let stand for up to 2 hours and then bake, uncovered, at 400° for 30 minutes, stirring 3 to 4 times. Toss with Parmesan, if desired, and serve immediately.

Serves 6 to 8

Vary this recipe by substituting whatever vegetables you have on hand!

Vegetable Pie

Crust

1½ **cups all-purpose flour**

1½ **teaspoons sugar**

2 **tablespoons milk**

½ **teaspoon salt**

½ **cup vegetable oil**

½ **cup Parmesan cheese, grated**

Filling

3 **cups broccoli florets**

½ **cup green onions, sliced**

2 **cups Monterey Jack cheese, shredded**

½ **cup Parmesan cheese, grated**

¼ **cup all-purpose flour**

½ **teaspoon dried thyme**

3 **tablespoons fresh basil, chopped, or 1 tablespoon dried**

¼ **teaspoon black pepper**

1 **large ripe tomato, thinly sliced**

1 **tablespoon butter, melted**

Combine crust ingredients and shape into a ball. Press dough into a 9-inch pie plate, covering bottom and sides.

Place broccoli in boiling water and simmer for 3 minutes. Plunge broccoli into cold water and drain well.

Combine onions, cheeses, flour, thyme, basil and pepper. Place half the cheese mixture into the pie shell. Layer broccoli on top of cheese and follow with tomato slices. Top with remaining cheese mixture. Drizzle with butter and bake, uncovered, at 350° until thoroughly cooked, about 30 minutes.

Serves 8

This recipe doubles as a vegetarian entrée or a colorful side dish. It may be assembled up to 4 hours early and baked just prior to serving.

Colorful Corn Sauté

vegetable cooking spray

2 cups fresh corn kernels, cut from cob or frozen corn kernels, thawed

1 cup green pepper (about 1), seeded and chopped

4 green onions, sliced diagonally in 1/2-inch pieces

1/4 cup fresh parsley, chopped, or 1 tablespoon dried

8 ounces cherry tomatoes, halved

1/2 teaspoon sugar

2 tablespoons white wine vinegar

1/2 teaspoon Dijon mustard

1 tablespoon fresh basil, chopped, or 1 teaspoon dried

1 tablespoon low-fat mayonnaise

1/4 teaspoon hot pepper sauce

Spray a non-stick skillet with cooking spray and heat to medium. Add corn, pepper and onions. Sauté until softened, about 5 minutes, stirring frequently.

Transfer vegetables to a bowl and stir in parsley and tomatoes.

Combine sugar, vinegar, mustard, basil, mayonnaise and hot pepper sauce in a small bowl and whisk together. Pour over corn mixture and toss well.

Serves 6

This versatile sauté is delicious served cold, room temperature, or hot.

Herbed Green Beans with Pine Nuts

1/3 cup pine nuts

1 pound fresh green beans, ends snapped

1/4 cup olive oil

1/4 cup tarragon vinegar

1 teaspoon dried oregano

1/2 teaspoon dried basil

1/2 teaspoon garlic salt

1/4 cup Parmesan cheese, grated

Toast pine nuts in a shallow pan at 350° for 15 minutes or until light brown.

Cook beans in boiling water until tender-crisp, about 5 minutes. Plunge in cold water, drain well and set aside.

Combine oil, vinegar and spices in a sauté pan over medium heat. When liquid is hot, add beans and nuts and heat thoroughly. Sprinkle with Parmesan and serve immediately.

Serves 4

These are delicious cold, too!

A Bundle of Beans

1 pound fresh green beans, ends snapped

8 strips of lean bacon, partially cooked

3 tablespoons butter

1 tablespoon onion, finely chopped

1 tablespoon white vinegar

1 tablespoon sugar

1/4 teaspoon salt

Cook beans in boiling water until tender-crisp, about 5 minutes. Plunge in cold water and drain well. Divide beans into 8 bundles and wrap each with a strip of bacon, securing with a toothpick. (Bundles may be made one day in advance.)

Place bundles on a baking sheet and bake at 400° for 10 to 15 minutes or until bacon is crisp.

Melt butter in a small skillet over medium heat, add onion and sauté until tender, about 3 minutes. Add vinegar, sugar and salt and heat thoroughly. Place bundles on serving platter and top with sauce.

Serves 8

Fabulous Four Pepper Stir-Fry

2 tablespoons lemon juice

1 1/2 tablespoons soy sauce

1 tablespoon honey

1/2 teaspoon chili oil or other hot sauce, optional

2 teaspoons vegetable oil

1 1/2 teaspoons fresh garlic, minced

1 1/2 teaspoons fresh or pickled ginger, minced

1 1/2 teaspoons jalapeño pepper, seeded and minced

2 tablespoons leeks or green onions, thinly sliced

4 cups red, yellow and green bell peppers, cored, seeded and cut into 1 1/2-inch squares

1 1/2 teaspoons cornstarch, dissolved in 1 tablespoon cold water

1 1/2 teaspoons sesame seeds, toasted

1 (10-ounce) package oriental egg noodles, cooked al dente, optional

Combine lemon juice, soy sauce, honey and chili oil, if desired, in a bowl and whisk until smooth. Set aside.

Heat a wok to high and swirl in oil. Add garlic, ginger, jalapeño and leeks and stir-fry until fragrant but not brown, about 15 seconds. Add peppers and stir-fry until peppers begin to soften, about 1 minute. Stir in lemon juice mixture and bring to a boil. Stir in cornstarch mixture and stir-fry for 30 seconds. Garnish with sesame seeds. Serve on top of oriental noodles, if desired.

Serves 4 to 6

Serve this as an attractive accompaniment to grilled or roasted meats.

Spicy Summer Cucumbers

2 tablespoons sugar

3/4 cup boiling water

1/2 cup white vinegar

3 cups cucumber, peeled and thinly sliced

1/2 cup carrot, shredded

1/4 cup green onions, thinly sliced

1/4 cup red bell pepper, chopped

2 tablespoons fresh cilantro, chopped

2 tablespoons fresh mint, chopped, optional

1 teaspoon fresh ginger, peeled and chopped

1 teaspoon serrano or jalapeño pepper, seeded and minced

1 clove garlic, chopped

1/2 teaspoon salt

Dissolve sugar in boiling water and add vinegar. Cover and refrigerate at least 2 hours.

Combine the remaining ingredients in a medium bowl. Pour chilled vinegar mixture over cucumber mixture and toss gently. Return to refrigerator and chill for 2 to 48 hours.

Drain liquid from cucumber mixture and serve.

Serves 4 to 6

If the cucumbers are waxed, be sure to peel them. If not, leave the skins on for the addition of color and benefit of vitamins.

DESSERTS

Blackberry Jam Cake
204

Honey Icing
204

Valentine Cake
205

Chocolate Marble Cake
206

Chocolate with a Conscience
207

I Wanna Banana Cake
208

Chocolate Steamed Pudding
209

Dark Chocolate Cheesecake
with Raspberries and Cream
210

Amaretto and Chocolate
Chip Cheesecake
211

Holiday Cheesecake
212

Blueberry Cream Pie
213

No-Fail Pie Crust
213

Northwest Huckleberry Pie
214

Rhubarb Meringue Pie
215

Chocolate Macadamia Tart
216

Coconut Pecan Torte
217

Chilled Amaretto Soufflé
218

Double Drizzled Pears
219

Surprise Packages
220

Snowcapped Cookies
221

Sour Cream Sugar Cookies
222

Lou's Ginger Cookies
222

Great Pumpkin Cookies
223

Cranberry and White
Chocolate Cookies
223

Not-Your-Average
Chocolate Chip Cookie
224

Arctic Apricot Squares
224

Apricot and Almond Biscotti
225

Babe Ruth Bars
226

Tantalizing Toffee Squares
226

Grandma's Candies
227

Almond Pecan Cashew Corn
227

Photo: Double Drizzled Pears and Dark Chocolate Cheesecake with Raspberries and Cream   Sponsor: Washington Trust Bank

Blackberry Jam Cake

1 cup butter, softened

2 cups sugar

4 large eggs at room
temperature, separated

1 cup seedless blackberry jam

3 cups all-purpose flour

1/2 teaspoon ground cloves

1/2 teaspoon nutmeg

1 teaspoon cinnamon

1 teaspoon baking soda

1 cup buttermilk

1 cup pecans or walnuts,
chopped, optional

1/2 teaspoon salt

Cream butter and sugar. Beat in egg yolks, one at a time. Add jam and beat well.

Sift flour with spices and baking soda. Add to butter mixture in 3 parts, alternating with buttermilk. Blend thoroughly with each addition, scraping down sides of bowl, but do not overbeat. Fold in nuts, if desired.

Beat egg whites and salt until stiff but not dry and gently fold into batter.

Butter and flour three 9-inch cake pans or one 10 x 12-inch pan. Pour batter into prepared pan(s). Bake at 325° for 30 to 35 minutes for layers, or 45 to 50 minutes for rectangle. Cool completely, remove from pan and frost with honey icing.

Serves 16

Honey Icing

1 (16-ounce) jar honey

3 egg whites

1/8 teaspoon salt

1/4 teaspoon almond extract

1/4 teaspoon vanilla extract

Place honey in a medium saucepan. Boil over medium heat without stirring for about 10 minutes or until it reaches thread stage (232°) on a candy thermometer.

Beat egg whites and salt until stiff but not dry. While continuing to beat, pour prepared honey into egg whites in a thin stream. Beat in almond and vanilla extracts. Spread between layers and on the top and sides of cake, creating pretty swirls and peaks.

Valentine Cake

Cake

1/2 cup butter, softened

1 1/2 cups sugar

2 eggs

2 1/2 cups self-rising flour

1 teaspoon baking soda

1 cup buttermilk

1 cup vegetable oil

2 ounces red food coloring

2 teaspoons unsweetened cocoa powder

1 teaspoon white vinegar

1 teaspoon vanilla

Frosting

1 cup butter, softened

4 ounces cream cheese, softened

3 cups powdered sugar

1 tablespoon vanilla

1 1/2 cups pecans, chopped

Cream the butter, sugar and eggs. Add remaining cake ingredients and mix with an electric mixer for one minute. Pour batter into two 9-inch cake pans which have been buttered and floured. Bake at 350° until toothpick inserted in center comes out clean, about 30 minutes. Let cake cool in pans for 15 minutes. Carefully remove from pans and cool completely. (Cakes may be made ahead and frozen for up to 2 weeks.)

For frosting, beat butter, cream cheese, powdered sugar and vanilla in a medium bowl until creamy. Fold in nuts and frost between layers and on top of cake. Keep refrigerated until 1 hour before serving.

Serves 10 to 12

This is an easy and delicious adaptation of red velvet cake - don't be afraid to put in all the food coloring!

Chocolate Marble Cake

2½ cups sugar, divided

3 eggs, divided

⅔ cup vegetable oil

3 cups all-purpose flour

2 teaspoons baking soda

½ cup unsweetened cocoa powder

2 cups water

2 tablespoons white vinegar

2 teaspoons vanilla

1 (8-ounce) package cream cheese, softened

6 ounces chocolate chips

Combine 2 cups sugar, 2 eggs and oil. Sift together flour, baking soda and cocoa. Combine water, vinegar and vanilla. Add half the flour mixture to the sugar mixture. Stir in half the water mixture. Repeat process and beat until smooth, about 3 minutes. Pour batter into an ungreased 9 x 13-inch pan.

Combine cream cheese, remaining 1/2 cup sugar and remaining egg. Mix until smooth. Stir in chocolate chips. Drop dollops of cream cheese mixture into the batter and swirl with a toothpick. Bake at 350° until cake tests done, about 1 hour.

Serves 10

To avoid splatters when using an electric mixer, place a paper plate on the bottom of the mixer. Punch holes in the plate for the beaters and insert. Splatters are stopped by the paper plate.

Chocolate with a Conscience

1 cup cake flour, sifted

1/3 cup unsweetened cocoa

1 teaspoon baking soda

1 teaspoon baking powder

6 large egg whites

1 1/3 cups brown sugar, packed

1 cup plain non-fat yogurt

1 teaspoon vanilla

vegetable cooking spray

powdered sugar

vanilla or cherry frozen yogurt

Combine flour, cocoa, baking soda and baking powder. Set aside.

Beat egg whites, brown sugar, yogurt and vanilla in a large bowl until well-blended. Stir in flour mixture and beat until evenly moistened.

Pour batter into an 8-inch square pan which has been sprayed with cooking spray and lightly dusted with flour. Bake at 350° for 30 to 40 minutes or until cake springs back when lightly touched in center.

Remove cake from oven and cool for 15 minutes. Invert onto serving plate and dust with powdered sugar. Serve with vanilla or cherry frozen yogurt.

Serves 8

For a change of pace, dust your cake pans with cocoa powder instead of flour when preparing a chocolate cake.

I Wanna Banana Cake

2¹/₃ cups whole wheat flour

2¹/₄ teaspoons baking soda, divided

¹/₂ teaspoon cream of tartar

³/₄ teaspoon cinnamon

dash nutmeg

1¹/₂ cups honey

¹/₃ cup maple syrup

1 teaspoon vanilla

1¹/₂ cups (about 3) mashed bananas

1 cup boiling water

1 cup dates, chopped

4 egg whites

vegetable cooking spray

Stir together flour, 3/4 teaspoon baking soda and spices in a large mixing bowl.

Combine honey, maple syrup, vanilla and banana in another bowl. Stir into flour mixture just until blended.

Place water, dates and remaining 1 1/2 teaspoons baking soda into a blender and process on high speed until dates are puréed. Stir into flour mixture.

Beat egg whites until foamy and gently fold into batter. Be careful not to over-mix. Spoon batter into a 9 x 13-inch pan which has been sprayed with cooking spray. Bake at 350° until cake tests done, about 35 to 40 minutes.

Serves 10 to 12

This cake is great with a light dusting of powdered sugar or frosted with the Honey Icing on page 204.

Chocolate Steamed Pudding

1 egg

1/2 cup butter, softened

1/2 cup sugar

1 1/2 ounces unsweetened chocolate, melted and cooled to room temperature

1 teaspoon vanilla

1 1/4 cups all-purpose flour

1/2 teaspoon salt

1 teaspoon baking powder

1/2 cup milk

Sauce

1 cup whipping cream

1 cup powdered sugar

1/4 cup butter, melted and cooled to room temperature

1 teaspoon vanilla

cocoa powder, optional

Beat egg with a whisk. Cream butter and sugar in a medium bowl. Add the whisked egg to the butter mixture. Stir in the melted chocolate and vanilla. Sift together flour, salt and baking powder. Alternately add the flour mixture and the milk to the chocolate mixture until blended. Batter will be thick.

Pour batter into a 1-quart (at least 4 inches high and 8 inches wide) covered baking dish which has been buttered and floured. Place lid on dish or cover with foil and secure the edges with string. Fill a large covered Dutch oven, steamer pot or turkey roaster with enough water to come to within 1 inch of the top of the baking dish. Place covered baking dish in pot, cover pot and bake at 350° until firm, about 1 hour.

Remove from oven and gently invert pudding on a serving plate.

To prepare the sauce, beat the cream until almost stiff. Add sugar, butter and vanilla. Beat until well-blended but not stiff. Pour sauce over pudding and allow to run down the sides or pour sauce on individual plates and place a slice of pudding on sauce. Top with cocoa powder, if desired.

Serves 8

Dark Chocolate Cheesecake with Raspberries and Cream

Crust

2½ **cups chocolate wafer cookies, finely crushed**

½ **cup butter, melted**

2 **tablespoons sugar**

1 **teaspoon instant coffee granules, optional**

Filling

8 **ounces semi-sweet chocolate**

3 **(8-ounce) packages cream cheese, softened**

¾ **cup sugar**

3 **large eggs, at room temperature**

2 **teaspoons vanilla**

2 **teaspoons instant coffee granules**

1 **cup sour cream at room temperature**

Topping

1 **cup fresh raspberries**

1 **cup whipping cream, whipped**

Combine crust ingredients and press into the bottom and sides of a well-greased 9-inch springform pan. Crumbs should go up to rim of the pan.

Melt chocolate and set aside. Beat cream cheese and sugar until it is smooth and very light. Beat in the eggs, vanilla and coffee granules. Stir in the melted chocolate and the sour cream and blend well. Mixture should be fluffy and brown in color.

Pour mixture into the prepared pan and bake in the middle of the oven at 300° for 1 hour and 15 minutes. The batter will fill up the entire pan but will not overflow in the oven and should puff up slightly in the middle. After baking time has elapsed, turn off oven and let cheesecake cool in the oven for 2 hours. Open the oven periodically to let some of the heat out to prevent cheesecake from falling. Cover tightly and chill 12 hours or until middle is completely set.

When ready to serve, run a knife gently around the edge to loosen crust. Remove sides of springform pan. Place on a serving plate and top with raspberries surrounded by whipped cream.

Serves 12

Amaretto and Chocolate Chip Cheesecake

Crust

1 cup semi-sweet chocolate chips

1 tablespoon unsalted butter

1 1/4 cups vanilla wafer crumbs

1/4 cup almonds, chopped

3 tablespoons powdered sugar

Filling

3 (8-ounce) packages cream cheese, softened

1 cup sugar

4 eggs at room temperature

1/4 cup Amaretto or other almond flavored liqueur

2 tablespoons cornstarch

1 teaspoon vanilla

1 cup high quality semi-sweet chocolate chips

Topping

2 cups sour cream at room temperature

1/4 cup sugar

1 teaspoon Amaretto or other almond flavored liqueur

1/2 cup sliced almonds, toasted

Remove the ring of a 9-inch springform pan and line bottom with foil, wrapping the extra underneath. Carefully replace the ring, lightly butter the foil and sides of pan.

For the crust, melt chocolate chips and butter over boiling water in a double boiler, stirring frequently until smooth. Remove top part from double boiler and allow chocolate to cool until tepid, about 8 minutes.

Stir together crumbs, almonds and powdered sugar until combined. Add the melted chocolate and stir together with a fork until well-blended. Press into the bottom and 1 inch up the sides of the pan.

For the filling, beat the cream cheese and 1 cup of sugar for 2 to 3 minutes or until smooth. Add eggs, one at a time, beating well after each addition. Add 1/4 cup liqueur, cornstarch and vanilla and beat until smooth. Stir in chocolate chips. Gently pour the filling into the crust. Bake at 375° for 50 to 60 minutes or until knife inserted into the center comes out clean. Cool for 5 minutes.

For the topping, combine the sour cream, 1/4 cup sugar and 1 teaspoon liqueur. Spread evenly over the surface of the warm cheesecake. Return to oven for 5 minutes. Remove from oven, cool and refrigerate overnight.

Remove the ring from the springform pan. Gently slide foil and cake off bottom of pan. Gently slide cake off foil and set on serving platter. Sprinkle with almonds.

Serves 12

Holiday Cheesecake

Cranberry sauce

   12 **ounces (about 3 1/2 cups)
       fresh or frozen cranberries**

    1 **cup sugar**

  1/4 **cup fresh orange juice**

Crust

 1 1/3 **cups vanilla wafer crumbs**

  1/4 **cup unsalted butter, melted**

Filling

    4 **(8-ounce) packages cream
       cheese, softened**

 1 1/3 **cups sugar**

    4 **large eggs at room temperature**

Topping

    2 **cups sour cream**

  1/3 **cup sugar**

    1 **teaspoon vanilla**

For the sauce, combine ingredients in a medium, heavy saucepan. Bring to a boil over medium-high heat, stirring until sugar dissolves. Reduce heat and simmer until berries pop and mixture thickens, stirring frequently, about 10 minutes. Cool completely.

For the crust, combine crumbs and butter until evenly moistened. Press crumb mixture onto the bottom of a lightly buttered 9-inch springform pan.

For the filling, beat cream cheese and sugar in a large bowl with an electric mixer until very smooth. Add eggs one at a time, beating after each addition until just blended. Spoon cheese filling onto crust.

Spoon 1 cup of the cranberry sauce over the cheese filling. Using a small sharp knife swirl to form marble pattern. Bake on center rack of oven at 350° until center is set, about one hour. Transfer cheesecake to rack and cool 30 minutes.

For the topping, mix sour cream, sugar and vanilla in medium bowl. Spoon over cheesecake. Return to oven at 350° and bake for 5 minutes. Transfer to rack and cool. Cover and refrigerate 6 to 7 hours or overnight. Serve with remaining cranberry sauce. (Cheesecake may be prepared 2 days ahead.)

Serves 12

Purchase fresh cranberries when they are readily available during the holiday season. Bags keep in the freezer for up to 6 months.

Blueberry Cream Pie

1 (9-inch) pie crust, unbaked

4 cups fresh blueberries

1¼ cups sugar, divided

2 tablespoons all-purpose flour

2 tablespoons cornstarch

1 (8-ounce) package cream cheese, softened

2 eggs

1 teaspoon vanilla

1 cup whipping cream, divided

Press pie crust into a 9-inch pie plate and flute edges. Combine blueberries, 1 cup sugar, flour and cornstarch. Stir, slightly mashing blueberries, until there is enough juice to absorb all the dry ingredients. Pour into pie crust and bake at 450° for 20 minutes.

Meanwhile, beat cream cheese and remaining 1/4 cup sugar until smooth. Beat in eggs, vanilla and 1/2 cup cream until combined. Remove pie from oven and pour mixture over the hot pie. Reduce heat to 350° and bake for an additional 45 minutes. Cover crust edges to prevent burning, if necessary. Whip remaining 1/2 cup cream. Serve pie warm or chilled with whipped cream.

Serves 8

No-Fail Pie Crust

1½ cups all-purpose flour

¼ teaspoon salt

½ cup shortening or butter, chilled and cut into pieces

3 to 4 tablespoons ice cold water

Stir together flour and salt. Cut shortening into flour mixture until it resembles the consistency of corn meal. Do not over-mix.

Sprinkle ice water onto dough and toss lightly. Push together to form a ball. Roll dough out on a lightly-floured surface to 1/8-inch thickness or the size of your pie plate plus 2 inches. Place dough into pie plate and gently press in place. Flute the edges by pinching together points every inch. To pre-bake, prick pastry every inch with a fork. Bake at 450° until golden brown, about 10 to 12 minutes.

Makes a single 9-inch pie crust

Chocolate Macadamia Tart

Crust

> 6 ounces (about 1⅓ cups) unsalted macadamia nuts

> ½ cup sugar

> 3 tablespoons unsalted butter, melted

Filling

> 12 ounces semi-sweet chocolate, chopped

> 1 cup whipping cream

> ⅓ cup sour cream

> ⅓ cup sugar

> 1 egg yolk

Sauce

> 1½ cups sugar

> ½ cup water

> 1 cup whipping cream

Topping

> 1 cup whipping cream, whipped

For the crust, combine nuts and sugar in food processor and process until finely chopped. Add melted butter and process until combined. Press mixture onto bottom and up sides of a 9-inch springform pan. Bake at 350° until golden, about 18 minutes. Cool on rack.

For the filling, melt chocolate in microwave at 50% power for 2 to 3 minutes, stirring every 30 seconds until smooth or melt in a double boiler. Set aside. Combine whipping cream, sour cream, sugar and egg yolk in a medium, heavy saucepan. Cook over medium heat stirring constantly until bubbles appear around edges. Do not boil. Gradually whisk cream mixture into melted chocolate. Pour filling into cooled crust. Refrigerate until set, at least 4 hours. (Can be prepared 1 day ahead. Cover tightly once set.)

For the sauce, heat sugar and water in a medium, heavy saucepan over medium heat, stirring until sugar dissolves. Increase heat to medium-high and boil, without stirring, until mixture is a rich amber color, about 10 minutes. Reduce heat to medium and add cream. The mixture will bubble. Cook, stirring occasionally, until caramel is smooth and slightly thickened, about 10 minutes. (Can be prepared 1 day ahead. Re-heat gently before serving.)

To serve, place 2 tablespoons of caramel sauce on plate. Top with slice of tart. Place dollop of whipped cream on each slice.

Serves 10

Coconut Pecan Torte

Crust

3/4 **cup powdered sugar**

1/2 **cup butter, softened**

1/4 **cup shortening**

1 1/2 **cups all-purpose flour**

Filling

2 **eggs, lightly beaten**

1 **cup brown sugar**

3/4 **cup pecans, chopped**

1 **cup coconut, shredded**

1/4 **cup all-purpose flour**

1/2 **teaspoon baking powder**

1/4 **teaspoon salt**

1/2 **teaspoon vanilla**

Blend powdered sugar, butter and shortening. Stir in flour and press onto the bottom of an ungreased quiche pan or 10-inch pie pan. Bake at 350° until crust is almost brown, about 12 minutes.

Combine filling ingredients and spread over the crust to 1/2 inch from the edge. Bake at 350° for 22 minutes. Cool. Serve with whipped cream or ice cream, if desired.

Serves 16

You can easily substitute walnuts or almonds for the pecans in this recipe.

Chilled Amaretto Soufflé

3 eggs, separated

1/2 cup sugar

1/4 cup Amaretto or other flavored liqueur

1 cup whipping cream

1 teaspoon vanilla

1 envelope unflavored gelatin

1/4 cup cold water

Sauce

1 (12-ounce) package frozen raspberries, thawed

1/4 cup powdered sugar

2 tablespoons Amaretto or other flavored liqueur

Beat egg yolks until lemon-colored and light, about 1 to 2 minutes. Add sugar and continue beating until creamy, about 2 minutes. Add 1/4 cup liqueur and set aside.

Beat egg whites in another bowl until stiff, but not dry and set aside.

Beat cream in a third bowl until soft peaks form. Beat in vanilla and set aside.

Soften gelatin in cold water for five minutes. Microwave until melted and thoroughly dissolved, about 1 to 2 minutes. Cool slightly.

Stir dissolved gelatin mixture into egg yolk mixture and combine thoroughly. Gently fold in beaten egg whites and whipped cream. Pour into an 8-inch soufflé dish or 8 individual ramekins and chill several hours or overnight.

For the sauce, place berries and their juice into a blender or processor. Add sugar and liqueur. Blend until smooth and thick. Strain sauce through cheesecloth or mesh strainer to remove seeds. Cover and chill.

To serve, place a portion of the soufflé in individual dessert bowls. Top with raspberry sauce or place sauce on top of individual ramekins. Serve with remaining sauce.

Serves 8

Grand Marnier, Frangelico and Chambourd are all inspiring adaptations!

Double Drizzled Pears

Pears

  6 **medium-sized ripe pears**

  3 **tablespoons lemon juice**

  3 **cups water**

  1/2 **large vanilla bean, split**

Chocolate Sauce

 2 1/2 **tablespoons sugar**

 2 1/2 **tablespoons unsweetened cocoa powder**

  2 **tablespoons water**

  2 **tablespoons light corn syrup**

 1/2 **teaspoon vanilla extract**

Raspberry Sauce

 1 1/4 **cups frozen unsweetened raspberries**

 2 1/2 **tablespoons sugar**

 1/2 **teaspoon cornstarch**

For the pears, slice 1/4-inch from the bottom of each pear so it will stand upright. Peel each pear and remove the core from the bottom end, leaving the stem intact. Combine the lemon juice, water and vanilla bean in a Dutch oven and bring to a boil over medium heat. Add pears cut side down. Cover, reduce heat and simmer until the pears are tender, about 20 minutes. Remove pears from liquid and cool.

For the chocolate sauce, combine sugar and cocoa in a saucepan and stir well. Add water and stir until smooth. Add corn syrup and stir well. Place over medium heat and bring to a boil, stirring constantly. Remove from heat and add the vanilla extract. Pour into a bowl, cover and chill.

For the raspberry sauce, combine the raspberries and sugar in a saucepan. Cook and stir over medium-low heat until the sugar dissolves, about 3 minutes. Strain raspberry mixture through a cheesecloth, discard seeds and return to saucepan. Add cornstarch and stir until dissolved. Place over medium heat and bring to a boil. Boil for 1 minute until slightly thickened. Remove from heat, pour into a bowl, cover and chill.

To serve, place 1 tablespoon raspberry sauce onto a dessert plate, place pear in center of sauce and drizzle with 1 tablespoon chocolate sauce.

Serves 6

Pears are usually sold while still green because they ripen better off the tree. To speed the process, place in a closed paper bag at room temperature for 3 to 7 days.

Surprise Packages

2 cups (about 2) apples, peeled, cored and cut into 1/2-inch chunks

2 cups (about 2) pears, peeled, cored and cut into 1/2-inch chunks

1 tablespoon water

8 prunes, pitted and cut into fourths

3/4 teaspoon cinnamon, divided

1/4 cup walnuts, chopped, optional

8 (12 x 16-inch) sheets phyllo dough, thawed

1 1/2 tablespoons butter, melted

4 (12-inch) pieces kitchen string

vegetable cooking spray

1 tablespoon powdered sugar

Place apples, pears and water in a saucepan. Cover and cook over low heat for 25 minutes. Uncover, add prunes and cook until all the juice has evaporated, about 5 minutes. Stir in 1/4 teaspoon cinnamon and walnuts, if desired. Remove from heat and cool.

Brush 1 sheet of phyllo with butter. Stack second sheet on top and brush with butter. Repeat with third sheet. Place fourth sheet on top, but do not brush with butter. Cut phyllo sheets in half. Spoon one-fourth of the fruit mixture in the center of each phyllo section. Gather edges of each section together and tie with string. Repeat with remaining 4 sheets of phyllo.

Place packages on a cookie sheet sprayed with cooking spray. Lightly brush with butter. Bake at 375° until lightly brown, about 16 minutes. Sift together remaining 1/2 teaspoon cinnamon and powdered sugar. Sprinkle over warm packets. Serve warm.

Serves 4

Snowcapped Cookies

2 cups all-purpose flour

1 teaspoon cinnamon

1/4 teaspoon salt

1/2 cup shortening

1/2 cup butter, softened

1/2 cup sugar

1/2 cup brown sugar

2 ounces unsweetened chocolate, melted and cooled

1 egg

1/2 cup dried cherries, chopped

6 ounces white chocolate, chopped

3 tablespoons shortening

Combine flour, cinnamon and salt and set aside. Beat shortening and butter on medium speed until soft. Add sugars and beat until fluffy. Add melted chocolate and egg and beat well. Stir in flour mixture and beat until combined. Gently stir in dried cherries. Cover dough and chill for at least one hour.

Shape dough into two 7-inch rolls, wrap with plastic wrap and chill for 6 to 24 hours. Unwrap rolls, slice into 1/4-inch slices, place on an ungreased cookie sheet and bake at 350° for 10 to 15 minutes. Remove to rack to cool.

Combine white chocolate and shortening in a microwave-safe bowl. Heat on high for 30 seconds and stir. Heat for an additional 30 seconds or until melted. Dip half of each cookie in the melted white chocolate and set on wax paper to cool.

Makes 3 1/2 dozen

To keep cookies soft, store them in a container with a tight-fitting lid. To keep cookies crisp, store them in a container with a loose-fitting lid.

Sour Cream Sugar Cookies

1 cup margarine, softened

2 cups sugar

1/2 teaspoon vanilla

2 eggs

1 cup sour cream

5 cups all-purpose flour

2 teaspoons baking powder

1 teaspoon baking soda

1 teaspoon salt

Cream margarine, sugar and vanilla. Beat eggs in a separate bowl until fluffy and add to the margarine mixture. Add sour cream and blend well. Add flour, baking powder, baking soda and salt. Mix well to moisten. Cover and refrigerate at least 1 hour or overnight.

Roll out dough and shape or cut into cookies. Sprinkle with decorative sprinkles, if desired. Bake at 375° on an ungreased cookie sheet until lightly browned, about 8 minutes. Remove to wire rack and cool. Frost if desired.

Makes 4 to 6 dozen

Lou's Ginger Cookies

1 3/4 cups sugar, divided

3/4 cup butter, softened

1 egg

1/4 cup light molasses

2 cups all-purpose flour

1 tablespoon baking soda

1/2 teaspoon salt

1 teaspoon ground cloves

1 teaspoon ground ginger

1 teaspoon cinnamon

Cream 1 cup sugar and butter together. Add the egg and molasses and blend well. Add the flour, baking soda, salt and spices. Mix well.

Shape dough into 1 1/2-inch balls. Roll each ball in remaining 3/4 cup sugar, place on an ungreased cookie sheet and flatten with palm or a flat-bottomed glass.

Bake at 350° for 8 to 10 minutes. Let cookies rest on the cookie sheet for 1 minute and then cool on racks.

Makes 18 cookies

Great Pumpkin Cookies

2 cups all-purpose flour

1 cup rolled oats

1 teaspoon baking soda

1 tablespoon cinnamon

1/2 teaspoon salt

1/2 cup butter, softened

1 cup brown sugar

1 cup sugar

1 egg

1 teaspoon vanilla

1 cup canned pumpkin

1 cup chocolate chips

Combine flour, oats, baking soda, cinnamon and salt. Set aside.

Cream butter in a large bowl and gradually add sugars, beating until light and fluffy. Add egg and vanilla and mix well. Alternately add the flour mixture and the pumpkin to the bowl with the butter, mixing well after each addition. Gently stir in the chocolate chips.

Drop rounded tablespoons of dough onto a lightly greased cookie sheet. Bake at 350° for 20 to 30 minutes until firm and lightly browned.

Makes 40 cookies

You may add 1 cup of chopped walnuts to this recipe.

Cranberry and White Chocolate Cookies

1 cup butter, softened

1 1/2 cups sugar

2 teaspoons baking soda

2 eggs

1 3/4 cups all-purpose flour

1 1/2 cups rolled oats

1 cup (6-ounces) white chocolate chips

1 1/2 cups fresh cranberries

Cream butter and sugar together in a medium bowl. Add baking soda and eggs and mix well. Add flour and oats and mix well. Fold in chips and cranberries and drop by heaping tablespoons onto a greased baking sheet.

Bake at 375° for 8 to 10 minutes or until done.

Makes 3 dozen cookies

Not-Your-Average Chocolate Chip Cookie

1/2 **cup butter, softened**

1/2 **cup oil**

1/2 **cup sugar**

1/2 **cup brown sugar**

1 **egg white**

1 1/2 **teaspoons vanilla**

1 3/4 **cups all-purpose flour**

1 **teaspoon salt**

1/2 **teaspoon baking soda**

1/2 **teaspoon cream of tartar**

3/4 **cup milk chocolate chips**

1/2 **cup crispy rice cereal**

1/2 **cup rolled oats**

1/2 **cup sliced almonds**

Cream together the butter, oil, sugars, egg white and vanilla. Sift together flour, salt, baking soda and cream of tartar in a separate bowl. Add the butter mixture and stir until combined. Fold in chocolate chips, cereal, oats and almonds.

Drop by heaping teaspoons onto an ungreased cookie sheet. Bake at 375° for 10 to 12 minutes. (The dough can be prepared ahead of time and stored in the refrigerator. The baked cookies freeze well.)

Makes 3 1/2 dozen

Substitute walnuts, pecans or peanuts or omit the nuts altogether!

Arctic Apricot Squares

1/2 **cup slivered almonds**

2 **cups vanilla wafers, crushed**

6 **tablespoons butter, melted**

2 **teaspoons almond extract**

4 **cups vanilla ice cream**

1 **cup apricot preserves**

Combine almonds, wafer crumbs, butter and extract in a large bowl. Press half of the crumb mixture into a 9 x 9-inch pan. Soften ice cream and gently spread 2 cups on top of the almond mixture, followed by a layer of preserves and a layer of the remaining ice cream. Top with remaining crumb mixture. Cover tightly and freeze until firm, at least 4 hours.

Serves 10 to 12

Apricot and Almond Biscotti

2³/₄ cups all-purpose flour

1¹/₂ cups sugar

¹/₂ cup unsalted butter, chilled and cut into pieces

2¹/₂ teaspoons baking powder

1 teaspoon salt

1 teaspoon ground ginger

²/₃ cup white chocolate chips

1²/₃ cups blanched slivered almonds, toasted

2 eggs

¹/₄ cup plus 1 tablespoon apricot brandy

2 tablespoons almond extract

1¹/₂ cups (6-ounces) dried apricots, diced

Combine flour, sugar, butter, baking powder, salt and ginger in a food processor and process until a fine meal forms, about 30 seconds. Add chips and process until finely chopped, about 30 seconds. Add almonds and chop coarsely, about 10 to 15 seconds.

Beat eggs, brandy and extract in a large bowl until blended. Add flour mixture and apricots and stir until a moist dough forms.

Line a cookie sheet with foil. Butter and flour foil. Divide dough into thirds and place on cookie sheet in three 12-inch strips. Moisten fingers and shape dough into 2-inch wide biscotti-shaped logs. Refrigerate 30 minutes.

Bake at 350° for 35 minutes. Remove logs from oven and cool. Cut each log into 3/4-inch slices and place each slice on its side on the baking sheet. Bake at 300° for 12 minutes. Turn biscotti and bake for an additional 12 minutes.

Makes 4 dozen

Biscotti, meaning cooked twice, is a traditional Italian dunking cookie. Serve this delectable treat with your mid-morning coffee or afternoon tea.

Babe Ruth Bars

1 cup light corn syrup

1 cup sugar

1½ cups creamy peanut butter

4 cups crispy rice cereal

¾ cup chocolate chips

¾ cup butterscotch chips

Combine corn syrup and sugar in a heavy saucepan and heat until mixture almost boils. Add peanut butter and stir until creamy and hot. Remove from heat and stir in crispy rice cereal. Spread evenly into a greased 9 x 13-inch pan.

Melt chocolate and butterscotch chips over low heat until smooth, stirring constantly. Spread on top of crispy rice mixture and refrigerate. Remove from refrigerator 30 minutes prior to serving and cut into bars.

Makes 24

Tantalizing Toffee Squares

1 cup butter, softened

1 cup brown sugar

1 egg yolk

1 teaspoon vanilla

1 cup all-purpose flour

6 (1½-ounce) milk chocolate bars, broken or 10 ounces milk chocolate chips

½ cup walnuts, pecans or almonds, coarsely chopped

Cream butter and sugar until smooth. Add egg yolk, vanilla and flour and beat until smooth. Spread to 1/4-inch thickness in an ungreased 15 1/2 x 10 1/2-inch pan with sides. Bake at 325° for 20 minutes or until done.

Remove from oven and immediately distribute chocolate pieces over top. Let melt and spread evenly over top. Sprinkle with nuts. Cool before cutting.

Makes 3 dozen

Grandma's Candies

1 (12-ounce) package
butterscotch chips

1/2 cup creamy or chunky
peanut butter

Place butterscotch chips in a microwave-safe bowl. Microwave, uncovered, for 30 seconds. Stir and continue to cook in 30-second increments, stirring each time, until the chips start to melt. Mix in peanut butter and return to microwave. Cook as before until mixture is fully melted and blended. Drop by teaspoons onto wax paper. Cool until firm, about 15 to 20 minutes. Store in an airtight container. These freeze well.

Makes 4 dozen (1-inch) candies

Don't let the ease of these candies fool you . . . they are delicious!

Almond Pecan Cashew Corn

3/4 cup shelled pecan halves

3/4 cup shelled whole almonds

1/2 cup whole cashews, roasted
and salted

8 cups popped white corn,
without salt or butter

1 cup sugar

1/2 cup corn syrup

1/3 cup water

1 cup unsalted butter

Combine pecans, almonds and cashews and place on a cookie sheet. Toast nuts at 350° until lightly browned, about 8 minutes. Combine popcorn and nuts in a large bowl and set aside.

Combine sugar, corn syrup and water in a medium, heavy saucepan. Bring to a boil over high heat. Wash down any sugar crystals which cling to the sides of the pan with a pastry brush dipped in cold water. Add butter and cook until candy thermometer registers 300°, stirring constantly. Lower heat to prevent burning, if necessary.

Pour hot syrup over popcorn mixture. Quickly toss to distribute syrup evenly. Spread popcorn on a greased baking sheet. Cool completely. Break into bite-sized pieces and store in plastic bags.

Makes 15 cups

Gold'n Delicious Committee

Chairmen
Louise Everett
Kathy Friedlander
Kris Mason

Steering Committee
Donna Halvorson
Tana Rekofke
Carol Wilson

Editors
Kathy Friedlander
Donna Halvorson
Tana Rekofke

Category Committees

Appetizers & Beverages
Mary Garras - Leader
Sue Baglien
Kelli Beaulaurier
Dianne Douthitt
Lynn Leonard
Maria Markopoulos
Julie Mauer

Breads & Soups
Catherine Klingel - Leader
Molly Beil
Cathy Brett
Margaret Ann Fallquist
Jane Franks
Connie Shields
Janet Vaughn
Sara Wardrip

Salads
Karin Marchant - Leader
Margo Burnette
Nancy Cover
Rhonda Fischer
Paula Johnson
Marlo Maxwell
Ellen Moe
Molly Preston
Elizabeth Schultheis

Pastas
Carmen Green - Leader
Maureen Cassidy
Barrie Estabrook
Doris Guelich
Brenda Larison
Catherine O'Connell
Leigh Phillips

Poultry, Fish & Seafood
Carol Weigand - Leader
Louise Everett
Cathy Heutmaker
Ruth Siegel Johnson
Robin Johnston
Gina Peterson
Gail Stevenson
Kristen Stevenson
Shellie Witter

Meats
Eleanor Andersen - Leader
Kristi Blake
Kris Mason
Ann Porter Brown
Tammy Tracy

Vegetables & Side Dishes
Bridget Piper - Leader
Mary Jane Broom
Janece Connor
Carole Jones
Pam McLaughlin
Karen Robideaux

Desserts
Sheila Geraghty Leek - Leader
Laurie Bigej
Cynthia Bohrnsen
Heidi Davis
Laura Lawton-Forsyth

Gold'n Delicious Committee

Marketing

Bonnie Hodge
Melody Hunt
Judy Rogers
Nancy Slack
Kathleen Wilson

Underwriting

Kris Mason
Carla Percival

Proof Readers

Jane Baldwin
Kristi Blake
Clysie Brooks-Hammond
John Everett
Tessa Grossman
Ron Halvorson
Kathleen Johnson Hart
Suzanne Lynch
Debbie Oscarson
Molly Preston
Judy Rogers
Nancy Slack
Gail Stevenson
Carol Wilson

Sales Committee

Jean Auerbach
Sue Chapin
Danette Driscoll
Linda Grabicki
Kathleen Johnson Hart
Bonnie Hodge
Kari Jones
Shellie Witter

Committee Members

Sarah Beyersdorf
Cynthia Bohrnsen
Debora Brock
Dian Brutocao
Sue Chapin
Janie Hemingway
Donna Herak
Jan House
Robin Johnston
Jane MacPherson
Marlo Maxwell
Sheila McDonald
Pam Ness
Julie O'Callaghan
Catherine O'Connell
Stacey O'Sullivan
Mary O'Toole
Sarah Porter
Victoria Roberge
Judy Rogers
Joanne Shiosaki
Gaye Shumaker
Leslie Wester
Elizabeth Will

ACKNOWLEDGEMENTS

The Junior League of Spokane thanks its members, families and friends

who contributed to this book. We sincerely hope that no one has been missed.

Dale Abendroth-Lenski	Alison Burns	Pula Dezfuli	Candi Morton Gilchrist	Ruth Ann Johnson
Barbara Ackerman	Janet Camp	Leann Dineen	Lupe Gilmartin	Ruth Siegel Johnson
Julie Adelchmon	Maureen Cassidy	Merilee Dinneen	Leone Goodwater	Robin Johnston
Lynn Alexander	Deidre Chadderdon	Dianne Douthitt	Cheryl Grabicki	Carole Jones
Eleanor Andersen	Dan Chambers	Danette Driscoll	Christine Grant	Kari Jones
Rondi Anderson	Susan Chapin	Ann Driver	Carmen Green	Wendy Jones
Carol Annis	Nancy Chappell	Gail Duba	Maureen Green	Gina Josephson
Jean Auerbach	Faris Charbonneau	Sylvia Duff	Donna Greenough	Mary Ann Jurgensen
Sue Baglien	Luann Charon	Margaret Ellersick	Tessa Grossman	Kathy Keller
Leslie Baker	Carol Ann Christnacht	Diane Ellingwood	Doris Guelich	Jean Kendall
Jane Baldwin	Staci Clary	Linda Essex	Michele Guidice-Carrozzo	Melinda Kenney
Vicki Barnes	Julie Clausen	Barrie Estabrook	Donna Halvorson	Sue Kibbey
Leslie Barrett	Mia Clausen	Louise Everett	Valerie Hamacher	Lynn Kimmel
Lori Beaty	Hazel Clemens	Jeanine Fagan	Susan Hamer	Mary Jo King
Kelli Beaulaurier	Judy Clemenson	Margaret Ann Fallquist	Tammie Hanson	Sue King
Molly Beil	Jan Coburn	Ann Fennessy	Andi Hart	Catherine Klingel
Sarah Beyersdorf	Peggy Codd	Joanne Ferris	Kathleen Johnson Hart	Clare Kobluk
Laurie Bigej	Deborah Johnston Coleman	Mickie Fichtner	Tracy Hattamer	Kathleen Kozlowski
Helen Biggs	Janece Connor	Noreen Filippi	Sherie Heimbigner	Marti Kransberger
Kristi Blake	Ellena Conway	Rhonda Fischer	Cathy Heutmaker	Mary Kuney
Theresa Blohowiak	Shawn Cooney	Elizabeth Fitzgerald	Bonnie Hodge	Barbara Kuuskvere
Toni Boggan	Beverly Corliss	Kelly Fitzgerald	Gary Hodge	Brenda Larison
Cynthia Bohrnsen	Nancy Cover	Helen Fosseen	Barbara Hoffman	Laura Lawton-Forsyth
Marylou Bonanzino	Karal Cox	Jane Franks	Marie Peterson Holland	Ray Lawton
Cathy Brett	Alanna Crouch	Merilee Frets	Wendy Holt	Donna Lee
Debora Brock	Sarah Crowther	Bill Friedlander	Jan House	Sheila Geraghty Leek
Clysie Brooks-Hammond	Christine Crummer	Kathy Friedlander	Jeni Hubbs	Stephanie Leek
Beverly Brown	Christi Culp	Rick Friedlander	Cathy Hughes	Lynn Leonard
Sally Brucker	Dottie Cummings	Robin Friedlander	Janet Huizinga	Haideh Lightfoot
Jennifer Brumblay-Dailey	Linda Cunningham	Sally Friedlander	Melody Hunt	Regina Lillie
Dian Brutocao	Candace Dahlstrom	Debbie Fucile	Diana Hyland	Nancy Lindsay
Bette Jo Buhler	Cindy Dandoy	Mary Garras	Vanpen Jenson	Gloria Lopez
Patti Buller	Heidi Davis	Marny Gaylord	Frank Johnson	Kim Louthian
Sylvia Bumgarner	Marcia Davis	Jack Geraghty	Linda Johnson	Beth Love
Jodi Burke	Marge Davis	Marlene Geraghty	Paula Johnson	Sally Love
Margo Burnette	Shelly Dawson	Lisa Giddings	Ruth Johnson	Dianne Loy Ferri

ACKNOWLEDGEMENTS

Megan Lynch
Molly Lynch
Elizabeth Maher
Lori Mai
Lynn Mandyke
Regina Manser
Karin Marchant
Maria Markopoulos
Deborah Martin
Kris Mason
Marge Mason
Warren Mason
Karen Matthews
Julie Mauer
Marlo Maxwell
Sheila McDonald
Bobbie McGann
Lynette McGarry
Pam McLaughlin
Barbara Meadors
Beth Merck
Angela Merritt
Julie Meyer
Robin Mickelson
Melanie Mikkelsen
Dorothy Miller
Joyce Miller
Patty Minnihan
Ellen Moe
Heidi Moore
Joy Moore
Peter Moye
Mary Mullendore
Kolleen Murray
Muffy Murphy
Sandy Nadeau
Pamela Ness
Lee Nielsen
Viviana Novillo
Karen Nyquist

Maureen O'Brien
Catherine O'Connell
Stacy O'Sullivan
Mary O'Toole
Cathy Oliver
Judith Onthank
Jodie Orcutt
Anne Orsi
Debbie Oscarson
Kathy Ossello
Grace Millay Ott
Cindy Paap
Elizabeth Palma
Dana Papesh
Julie Payne
Carla Percival
Else Marie Petersen
Gina Peterson
Marie Peterson Holland
LaDonna Petrettee
Joanne Pettit
Karen Peven
Claudia Phenneger
Leigh Phillips
Marion Phillips
Bridget Piper
Jane Piston
Debra Poffenroth
Deborah Poppy
Sarah Porter
Ann Porter Brown
Molly Preston
Bonnie Quist
Nancy Rector
Judy Reed
Caren Reeves
Tana Rekofke
Kathy Reugh
Caroll Ritter
Mary Ritter Heitkemper

Stacy Ritter
Victoria Roberge
Karen Robideaux
Judy Rogers
Janet Ruehl
Marilyn Sandberg
Karen Schmirler
Sherry Schnell
Jenny Schuetzle
Catherine Schultheis
Elizabeth Schultheis
Edie Schurra
Nancy Seefried
Sue Ellen Seefried
Stephanie Seely
Connie Shields
Joanne Shiosaki
Gaye Shumaker
Jan Sims
Nancy Slack
Jacque Smith
Lori Smith
Robin Smith
Sue Smith
Julie Smitherman
Laurie Snover
Heidi Stanley
Marilyn Stedman
Louise Sterling
Karen Stevens
Gail Stevenson
Kristen Stevenson
Lorna Stevenson
Richard Stevenson
Wendy Stevenson
John Stoianoff
LuAnn Stone
Laurie Stupakis
Suzie Swenson
Ashley Talarico

Victoria Taylor
Audrey Thayer
Kimberly Thielman
Karen Thomas
Regina Thomas
Shannon Kwasney Thomas
Susan Thomson
Ainslie Toole
Tammy Tracy
Julie Travis
Carolyn Treloar
Susanne Treloar
Marianne Treppiedi
Margaret Tyler
Jan Tyson
Nancy Unger
Janet Vaughn
Amelia Velis
Carole Walker
Nancy Sue Wallace
Sara Wardrip
Wendy Watcher
Peggy Weatherman
Carol Weigand
Ginger West
Leslie Wester
Alesha Wiese
Betsy Wilkerson
Elizabeth Will
Jill Williams
Carol Wilson
Danelle Wilson
Kathleen Wilson
Mary Wilson
Rosanne Winters
Shellie Witter
Ileana Wood
Betsy Wooten
Pamela Yamayee
Debra Yaritz

Index

A

A Bundle of Beans, 199

A Perfect Ten, 150

Almond Pecan Cashew Corn, 227

Amaretto and Chocolate Chip Cheesecake, 211

Angel Hair Pasta with Crab and Pesto, 105

Appetizers
Artichoke Relish with Pita Chips, 33
Best-of-the-Best Artichoke Dip, 34
Black Bean Salsa, 29
Bleu Ribbon Dip, 30
Blind Date Dip, 35
Citrus-Sauced Crab Cakes, 14
Confetti Relish, 32
Dill Dip with a Twist, 30
Fabulous Fruit Dip, 36
Fontina Quesadillas, 34
Frosted Spinach Torte, 21
Garden Herb Cheese Spread, 31
Glazed Shrimp Kabobs, 17
Joanne's Spicy Shrimp Salsa, 28
Korean Beef, 25
Lamb and Melon Kabobs, 24
Layered Tomato Pesto, 17
Mediterranean Skewers, 23
Party Bread, 27
Peppy Pecans, 36
Phyllo-Wrapped Brie with Red Pepper Jelly, 19
Rave Reviews Dip, 31
Red Pepper Jelly, 19
Roasted Red Pepper Crostini, 28
Salmon Tartlets, 13
Seafood Pepper Strips, 15
Shrimp and Tortellini Kabobs, 16
Smoked Salmon with Apples, 12
Smoked Turkey in Endive, 26
Spinach and Feta Mushroom Caps, 22
Steamed Clams with Sherry and Herbs, 18
Walla Walla Sweet Squares, 20

Apple Cider Surprise, 37

Apple Streusel Pizza, 49

Apples
Apple Cider Surprise, 37
Apple Streusel Pizza, 49
Chicken Breasts with Apple Cream Sauce, 140
Cider Glazed Ham with Golden Delicious Apples, 172
Greenbluff Apple Soup, 77
Magnificent Apple Muffins, 42
Northwest Huckleberry Pie, 214

Smoked Salmon with Apples, 12
Surprise Packages, 220
Washington Pork Chops, 176

Apricots
Apricot and Almond Biscotti, 225
Arctic Apricot Squares, 224

Apricot and Almond Biscotti, 225

Arctic Apricot Squares, 224

Artichoke Relish with Pita Chips, 33

Artichokes
Artichoke Relish with Pita Chips, 33
Best-of-the-Best Artichoke Dip, 34
Cheese Filled Torta, 58
Sautéed Artichoke Hearts with Red Bell Peppers, 188

Arugula and Goat Cheese Salad, 97

Asian Steak Salad, 80

Asparagus
Asparagus Pignolias, 192
Marinated Asparagus, 191
New Potato & Asparagus Salad, 92
Orange-Glazed Asparagus, 192
Scallops with Asparagus in Parchment, 132

Asparagus Pignolias, 192

Autumn Salad with Spicy Walnuts, 99

B

Babe Ruth Bars, 226

Baby Pea Salad with Cashews, 92

Bacon Topped Focaccia, 60

Baked French Toast, 62

Baked Spinach Fettuccine, 110

Baked White Fish with Pesto, 132

Balsamic Grilled Chicken Breasts, 146

Banana Oatmeal Muffins, 44

Bananas
Banana Oatmeal Muffins, 44
I Wanna Banana Cake, 208

Barbecue Butter for Fish, 123

Bars
Arctic Apricot Squares, 224
Babe Ruth Bars, 226
Tantalizing Toffee Squares, 226

Basic Bread Dough, 54

Basil Mushroom Fettuccine with Tomato, 110

Basil Pesto, 105

Bay Scallop Chowder, 73

Beans, Black
Black Bean and Turkey Stew, 156
Black Bean Salsa, 29
Mexican Black Beans with Rice, 182
Mexican Skillet Chicken, 151

Beans, Green
A Bundle of Beans, 199
Herbed Green Beans with Pine Nuts, 199

Beef
Asian Steak Salad, 80
Best Focaccia Beef Sandwich, 171
Bleu Cheese Filets with Brandy Sauce, 161
Brandied Beef Stew, 168
Company's Coming Beef Rolls, 160
Crock Pot Beef Stroganoff, 169
Fantastic Filets, 162
Hearty Lasagna, 118
Herbed Tenderloin Steaks with Mustard Sauce, 163
Killer Flank Steak, 163
Korean Beef, 25
Mexican Shredded Beef, 166
Persian Skewers, 164
Robin's Chunky Chili, 167
Spicy Steak and Pasta Salad with Shiitake Mushrooms, 81
Tenderloin Deluxe, 161
The King of Italian Meat Sauces, 115
Two Pepper Steak, 165
Walla Walla Steak Sandwich with Horseradish Sauce, 170

Best Focaccia Beef Sandwich, 171

Best-of-the-Best Artichoke Dip, 34

Beverages
Apple Cider Surprise, 37
Bull's Eye Bloody Mary, 39
Conrad's Gin Fizz, 38
Cranberry Tea, 37
Golden Cooler, 38
Iced Spiked Coffee, 39

Black Bean and Turkey Stew, 156

Black Bean Salsa, 29

Blackberry Jam Cake, 204

Bleu Cheese
Bleu Cheese Filets with Brandy Sauce, 161
Bleu Ribbon Dip, 30

Bleu Cheese Filets with Brandy Sauce, 161

Bleu Ribbon Dip, 30

Index

Blind Date Dip, 35

Blueberry Cream Pie, 213

Brandied Beef Stew, 168

Breads, Sweet
    Raisin Oatmeal Bread, 50

Breads, Yeast
    Bacon Topped Focaccia, 60
    Basic Bread Dough, 54
    Cheese Filled Torta, 58
    Dill Onion Bread, 51
    Garlic Butter Buns, 56
    Golden Harvest Bread, 52
    Herb Rolls, 56
    Italian Breadsticks, 53
    Party Bread, 27
    Picnic Pizza Bread, 57
    Quick & Healthy Wheat Bread, 50
    Swiss Onion Bread Ring, 55

Breakfast
    Baked French Toast, 62
    No Guilt Strata, 64
    Pizza for Breakfast, 65
    Swiss Cheese Breakfast Bake, 63

Brie
    Focaccia Bread with Brie and Sun-Dried Tomatoes, 61
    Phyllo-Wrapped Brie with Red Pepper Jelly, 19

Broccoli
    The Ultimate Endive Salad, 98
    Vegetable Pie, 195

Browned Butter Sauce, 107

Buffy's Favorite Chicken, 146

Bulgar Salad with Lemon and Curry, 86

Bull's Eye Bloody Mary, 39

Burritos
    River Road Burritos with Avocado Salsa, 148

Buttermilk Bleu Salad Dressing, 100

Butter
    Barbecue Butter for Fish, 123
    Browned Butter Sauce, 107
    Scampi Butter, 126

C

Cabbage
    Kielbasa Cabbage Soup, 71

Cajun Linguine, 109

Cakes
    Blackberry Jam Cake, 204

Chocolate Marble Cake, 206
Chocolate with a Conscience, 207
I Wanna Banana Cake, 208
Valentine Cake, 205

Camp Jack Chicken, 145

Candy
    Almond Pecan Cashew Corn, 227
    Grandma's Candies, 227

Caribbean Snapper, 131

Carrot Soup with Coriander, 76

Carrots
    Carrot Soup with Coriander, 76
    Carrots for Kids, 196
    Mustard Dill Baby Carrots, 196

Carrots for Kids, 196

Cashew Chicken Salad with Oranges, 88

Catch & Keep Grilled Trout, 129

Cauliflower
    Sensational Cauliflower, 197

Celebration Potato Puffs, 186

Cheese Filled Torta, 58

Cheesecakes
    Amaretto and Chocolate Chip Cheesecake, 211
    Dark Chocolate Cheesecake with Raspberries and Cream, 210
    Holiday Cheesecake, 212

Cherry Scones, 46

Chicken
    Entrees
        A Perfect Ten, 150
        Balsamic Grilled Chicken Breasts, 146
        Buffy's Favorite Chicken, 146
        Cajun Linguine, 109
        Camp Jack Chicken, 145
        Chicken and Cheese Enchiladas, 147
        Chicken Breasts with Apple Cream Sauce, 140
        Cypress Chicken and Rice, 143
        Fiery Thai Style Pizza, 153
        Five Spice Stir-Fry, 152
        Herbed Chicken Fricassee, 141
        Lime Grilled Jalapeño Chicken, 147
        Mexican Skillet Chicken, 151
        No-Fuss Chicken, 144
        Open Sesame Chicken, 144
        Rick's Radio Roasted Chicken, 154
        River Road Burritos with Avocado Salsa, 148
        Smothered Chicken, 142
        Southwestern Grilled Chicken Sandwiches, 149

Spicy Ginger Garlic Chicken, 151
Thai Chicken Fettuccine, 108
Salads
    Cashew Chicken Salad with Oranges, 88
    Chutney Chicken Salad, 89
    Lemon Mint Chicken Salad, 90
Soups
    Thai Coconut Soup, 75
    Tortilla Soup, 72

Chicken and Cheese Enchiladas, 147

Chicken Breasts with Apple Cream Sauce, 140

Chilled Amaretto Soufflé, 218

Chilled Corn Soup, 77

Chocolate
    Amaretto and Chocolate Chip Cheesecake, 211
    Babe Ruth Bars, 226
    Chocolate Macadamia Tart, 216
    Chocolate Marble Cake, 206
    Chocolate Steamed Pudding, 209
    Chocolate with a Conscience, 207
    Cranberry and White Chocolate Cookies, 223
    Dark Chocolate Cheesecake with Raspberries and Cream, 210
    Not-Your-Average Chocolate Chip Cookie, 224
    Snowcapped Cookies, 221
    Tantalizing Toffee Squares, 226

Chocolate Macadamia Tart, 216

Chocolate Marble Cake, 206

Chocolate Steamed Pudding, 209

Chocolate with a Conscience, 207

Chutney
    Mango Chutney, 89

Chutney Chicken Salad, 89

Cider Glazed Ham with Golden Delicious Apples, 172

Cilantro Pesto Pasta, 111

Citrus Vinaigrette, 101

Citrus-Sauced Crab Cakes, 14

Clams
    Linguine with Garlic and Clam Sauce, 106
    Pacific Fresh Cioppino, 130
    Steamed Clams with Sherry and Herbs, 18

Coconut Pecan Torte, 217

Coffee Cakes
    Huckleberry Streusel Coffee Cake, 48
    Raspberry Kuchen, 47

Colorful Corn Sauté, 198

INDEX

Company's Coming Beef Rolls, 160

Confetti Relish, 32

Conrad's Gin Fizz, 38

Cookies
    Apricot and Almond Biscotti, 225
    Cranberry and White Chocolate Cookies, 223
    Great Pumpkin Cookies, 223
    Lou's Ginger Cookies, 222
    Not-Your-Average Chocolate Chip Cookie, 224
    Snowcapped Cookies, 221
    Sour Cream Sugar Cookies, 222

Cool Cucumber Soup, 76

Corn
    Chilled Corn Soup, 77
    Colorful Corn Sauté, 198
    Confetti Relish, 32
    Curried Pilaf with Corn, 181

Couscous
    Incredible Couscous Salad, 84
    Pilaf-Style Couscous, 183

Crab
    Angel Hair Pasta with Crab and Pesto, 105
    Citrus-Sauced Crab Cakes, 14
    Crab Stuffed Sole, 134
    Pacific Fresh Cioppino, 130
    Pacific Fresh Wild Rice Salad, 82
    Seafood Pepper Strips, 15

Crab Stuffed Sole, 134

Cranberries
    Cranberry and White Chocolate Cookies, 223
    Cranberry Pork Tenderloin, 174
    Cranberry Tea, 37
    Holiday Cheesecake, 212
    Wild Rice and Cranberry Pilaf, 180

Cranberry and White Chocolate Cookies, 223

Cranberry Pork Tenderloin, 174

Cranberry Tea, 37

Cream Cheese Crescents, 45

Crispy Crouton Salad, 87

Crock Pot Beef Stroganoff, 169

Crostini
    Roasted Red Pepper Crostini, 28

Cucumbers
    Cool Cucumber Soup, 76
    Spicy Summer Cucumbers, 201

Curried Pilaf with Corn, 181

Cypress Chicken and Rice, 143

D

Dark Chocolate Cheesecake with Raspberries and
    Cream, 210

Dill Dip with a Twist, 30

Dill Onion Bread, 51

Dips
    Artichoke Relish with Pita Chips, 33
    Best-of-the-Best Artichoke Dip, 34
    Bleu Ribbon Dip, 30
    Blind Date Dip, 35
    Confetti Relish, 32
    Dill Dip with a Twist, 30
    Fabulous Fruit Dip, 36
    Garden Herb Cheese Spread, 31
    Layered Tomato Pesto, 17
    Rave Reviews Dip, 31

Double Drizzled Pears, 219

E

Eggs
    No Guilt Strata, 64
    Pizza for Breakfast, 65
    Swiss Cheese Breakfast Bake, 63

Enchiladas
    Chicken and Cheese Enchiladas, 147

F

Fabulous Four Pepper Stir-Fry, 200

Fabulous Fruit Dip, 36

Fantastic Filets, 162

Favorite Fruit, 93

Fiery Thai Style Pizza, 153

Fish & Seafood
    Appetizers
        Citrus-Sauced Crab Cakes, 14
        Glazed Shrimp Kabobs, 17
        Joanne's Spicy Shrimp Salsa, 28
        Salmon Tartlets, 13
        Seafood Pepper Strips, 15
        Shrimp and Tortellini Kabobs, 16
        Smoked Salmon with Apples, 12
        Steamed Clams with Sherry and Herbs, 18
    Entrees
        Angel Hair Pasta with Crab and Pesto, 105
        Baked White Fish with Pesto, 132
        Barbecue Butter for Fish, 123

        Caribbean Snapper, 131
        Catch & Keep Grilled Trout, 129
        Crab Stuffed Sole, 134
        Ginger Garlic Shrimp, 127
        Ginger Halibut in Parchment, 137
        Golden Tequila Sauce for White Fish, 133
        Grilled Mahi Mahi with Mango Salsa, 136
        Grilled Salmon with Yogurt Dill Sauce, 123
        Indian Spiced Shrimp, 128
        Moroccan Fish, 131
        Salmon en Papillote, 122
        Salmon in Phyllo, 124
        Salmon with Ginger Butter, 125
        Sauced Shrimp, 125
        Scallops Fettuccine, 107
        Scallops with Asparagus in Parchment, 132
        Seasoned Stuffed Sole, 135
        Shrimp in Phyllo, 126
        Sun-Dried Scallop Sauté, 133
    Salads
        Greek Orzo Salad with Shrimp, 83
        Pacific Fresh Wild Rice Salad, 82
    Soups
        Bay Scallop Chowder, 73
        Pacific Fresh Cioppino, 130
        Shrimp and St. Maries Wild Rice Soup, 74

Five Spice Stir-Fry, 152

Focaccia
    Bacon Topped Focaccia, 60
    Best Focaccia Beef Sandwich, 171
    Focaccia Bread with Brie and Sun-Dried Tomatoes, 61

Focaccia Bread with Brie and Sun-Dried Tomatoes, 61

Fontina Quesadillas, 34

French Toast
    Baked French Toast, 62

Frosted Spinach Torte, 21

Frostings
    Honey Icing, 204

Fruit
    Fabulous Fruit Dip, 36
    Favorite Fruit, 93

G

Garden Herb Cheese Spread, 31

Garlic, Baked
    Blind Date Dip, 35

Garlic Butter Buns, 56

Garlic Mashed Potatoes, 184

INDEX

Ginger Garlic Shrimp, 127
Ginger Halibut in Parchment, 137
Glazed Shrimp Kabobs, 17
Golden Cooler, 38
Golden Harvest Bread, 52
Golden Raisin Scones, 47
Golden Tequila Sauce for White Fish, 133
Gorgonzola Cheese
    Red Pepper and Gorgonzola Lasagna, 119
    Romaine, Gorgonzola and Walnut Salad, 91
Grandma's Candies, 227
Great Pumpkin Cookies, 223
Greek Orzo Salad with Shrimp, 83
Greenbluff Apple Soup, 77
Greens with Huckleberry Vinaigrette, 100
Grilled Mahi Mahi with Mango Salsa, 136
Grilled Salmon with Yogurt Dill Sauce, 123

H
Halibut
    Ginger Halibut in Parchment, 137
Hearty Lasagna, 118
Heavenly Marinara, 104
Herb Roasted Vegetables, 194
Herb Rolls, 56
Herbed Chicken Fricassee, 141
Herbed Green Beans with Pine Nuts, 199
Herbed Potatoes in Parchment, 188
Herbed Tenderloin Steaks with Mustard Sauce, 163
Holiday Cheesecake, 212
Honey Icing, 204
Honey Mustard Dressing, 101
Huckleberries
    Greens with Huckleberry Vinaigrette, 100
    Huckleberry Streusel Coffee Cake, 48
    Huckleberry Drizzle Salad, 94
    Huckleberry Pork Chops, 177
    Northwest Huckleberry Pie, 214
Huckleberry Streusel Coffee Cake, 48
Huckleberry Drizzle Salad, 94
Huckleberry Pork Chops, 177

I
I Wanna Banana Cake, 208
Iced Spiked Coffee, 39
Incredible Couscous Salad, 84
Indian Spiced Shrimp, 128
Italian Breadsticks, 53
Italian Sausage and Bean Soup, 70
Italian Sausage Pasta, 114
Italian Spinach Sauté, 191

J
Jelly
    Red Pepper Jelly, 19
Jicama Orange Salad, 95
Joanne's Spicy Shrimp Salsa, 28

K
Kielbasa Cabbage Soup, 71
Killer Flank Steak, 163
Korean Beef, 25

L
Lamb
    Lamb and Melon Kabobs, 24
    New Zealand BBQ Leg of Lamb, 171
Lamb and Melon Kabobs, 24
Lasagna
    Hearty Lasagna, 118
    Red Pepper and Gorgonzola Lasagna, 119
Layered Tomato Pesto, 17
Lemon Mint Chicken Salad, 90
Lemon Muffins with Walnuts, 43
Light & Fluffy Sweet Potato Soufflé, 187
Lime Grilled Jalapeño Chicken, 147
Linguine with Garlic and Clam Sauce, 106
Lite 'n Hearty
    Appetizers
        Artichoke Relish with Pita Chips, 33
        Black Bean Salsa, 29
        Confetti Relish, 32
        Fabulous Fruit Dip, 36
        Joanne's Spicy Shrimp Salsa, 28
        Roasted Red Pepper Crostini, 28

Beverages
    Apple Cider Surprise, 37
    Cranberry Tea, 37
    Golden Cooler, 38
Breads
    Banana Oatmeal Muffins, 44
    Basic Bread Dough, 54
    Dill Onion Bread, 51
    Golden Harvest Bread, 52
    Herb Rolls, 56
    Italian Breadsticks, 53
    Magnificent Apple Muffins, 42
    Quick & Healthy Wheat Bread, 50
    Raisin Oatmeal Bread, 50
    Swiss Onion Bread Ring, 55
Breakfasts
    No Guilt Strata, 64
Desserts
    Chocolate with a Conscience, 207
    Double Drizzled Pears, 219
    I Wanna Banana Cake, 208
    Surprise Packages, 220
Entrees
    A Perfect Ten, 150
    Balsamic Grilled Chicken Breasts, 146
    Black Bean and Turkey Stew, 156
    Brandied Beef Stew, 168
    Buffy's Favorite Chicken, 146
    Cajun Linguine, 109
    Caribbean Snapper, 131
    Cilantro Pesto Pasta, 111
    Crab Stuffed Sole, 134
    Cypress Chicken and Rice, 143
    Fabulous Four Pepper Stir-Fry, 200
    Fiery Thai Style Pizza, 153
    Ginger Halibut in Parchment, 137
    Golden Tequila Sauce for White Fish, 133
    Grilled Mahi Mahi with Mango Salsa, 136
    Hearty Lasagna, 118
    Heavenly Marinara, 104
    Herbed Chicken Fricassee, 141
    Huckleberry Pork Chops, 177
    Indian Spiced Shrimp, 128
    Linguine with Garlic and Clam Sauce, 106
    Mexican Skillet Chicken, 151
    Moroccan Fish, 131
    Persian Skewers, 164
    Rick's Radio Roasted Chicken, 154
    Smothered Chicken, 142

INDEX

Southwestern Grilled Chicken Sandwiches, 149
Spicy Ginger Garlic Chicken, 151
The King of Italian Meat Sauces, 115
Two Pepper Steak, 165
Washington Pork Chops, 176

Salads
Bulgar Salad with Lemon and Curry, 86
Chutney Chicken Salad, 89
Favorite Fruit, 93
Incredible Couscous Salad, 84
Lemon Mint Chicken Salad, 90
Mango Chutney, 89
Pacific Fresh Wild Rice Salad, 82
Spinach Salad with Papaya Salsa, 96

Soups
Bay Scallop Chowder, 73
Greenbluff Apple Soup, 77
Thea's Bean Soup, 69
Tortilla Soup, 72
Tuscan Soup, 68

Vegetables & Side Dishes
Colorful Corn Sauté, 198
Curried Pilaf with Corn, 181
Herbed Potatoes in Parchment, 188
Light & Fluffy Sweet Potato Soufflé, 187
Mexican Black Beans with Rice, 182
Mustard Dill Baby Carrots, 196
New Potatoes with Herbed Shallot Butter, 185
New Potatoes and Leeks Dijon, 185
Orange-Glazed Asparagus, 192
Rice Pilaf with Mushrooms and Pecans, 182
Sautéed Artichoke Hearts with Red Bell
    Peppers, 188
Sautéed Mushrooms with Sherry, 189
Spicy Summer Cucumbers, 201

Lou's Ginger Cookies, 222

M

Magnificent Apple Muffins, 42

Mahi Mahi
Grilled Mahi Mahi with Mango Salsa, 136

Mama B's Baked Ziti, 117
Mango Chutney, 89
Marinated Asparagus, 191
Marinated Pork Tenderloin, 175
Mediterranean Skewers, 23
Mexican Black Beans with Rice, 182
Mexican Shredded Beef, 166

Mexican Skillet Chicken, 151
Moroccan Fish, 131

Muffins
Banana Oatmeal Muffins, 44
Lemon Muffins with Walnuts, 43
Magnificent Apple Muffins, 42
Pecan Mini-Muffins, 43

Muffuletta, 59
Mushroom Soup with Cashews, 74

Mushrooms
Basil Mushroom Fettuccine with Tomato, 110
Mediterranean Skewers, 23
Mushroom Soup with Cashews, 74
Palouse Pheasant with Mushroom Sauce, 155
Rice Pilaf with Mushrooms and Pecans, 182
Sautéed Mushrooms with Sherry, 189
Spicy Steak and Pasta Salad with Shiitake
    Mushrooms, 81
Spinach and Feta Mushroom Caps, 22
Washington Wild Rice, 180

Mustard Dill Baby Carrots, 196

N

New Potato & Asparagus Salad, 92
New Potatoes with Herbed Shallot Butter, 185
New Potatoes and Leeks Dijon, 185
New Zealand BBQ Leg of Lamb, 171
No-Fail Pie Crust, 213
No-Fuss Chicken, 144
No Guilt Strata, 64
Northwest Huckleberry Pie, 214
Not-Your-Average Chocolate Chip Cookie, 224

O

One at a Thyme Spinach Soufflés, 190
One Hundred and One Zucchini, 193

Onions
Walla Walla Steak Sandwich with Horseradish
    Sauce, 170
Walla Walla Sweet Squares, 20

Open Sesame Chicken, 144
Orange-Glazed Asparagus, 192
Oriental Glazed Spareribs, 177
Orzo with Parmesan and Pesto, 183

P

Pacific Fresh Cioppino, 130
Pacific Fresh Wild Rice Salad, 82
Palouse Pheasant with Mushroom Sauce, 155
Paradise Rice with Bean Sprouts, 181
Party Bread, 27

Pasta
Angel Hair Pasta with Crab and Pesto, 105
Baked Spinach Fettuccine, 110
Basil Mushroom Fettuccine with Tomato, 110
Browned Butter Sauce, 107
Cajun Linguine, 109
Cilantro Pesto Pasta, 111
Hearty Lasagna, 118
Heavenly Marinara, 104
Italian Sausage Pasta, 114
Linguine with Garlic and Clam Sauce, 106
Mama B's Baked Ziti, 117
Orzo with Parmesan and Pesto, 183
Pasta Pancetta, 113
Pilaf-Style Couscous, 183
Popeye's Mostaccioli, 113
President's Cannelloni, 116
Red Pepper and Gorgonzola Lasagna, 119
Scallops Fettuccine, 107
Thai Chicken Fettuccine, 108
The King of Italian Meat Sauces, 115
Tortellini Primavera, 112

Pasta Pancetta, 113

Pears
Double Drizzled Pears, 219

Peas
Baby Pea Salad with Cashews, 92

Pecans
Almond Pecan Cashew Corn, 227
Coconut Pecan Torte, 217
Pecan Mini-Muffins, 43
Peppy Pecans, 36
Rice Pilaf with Mushrooms and Pecans, 182

Pecan Mini-Muffins, 43

Pepperoni
Party Bread, 27
Picnic Pizza Bread, 57

Peppers, Bell
Fabulous Four Pepper Stir-Fry, 200
Herb Roasted Vegetables, 194
Mediterranean Skewers, 23
Red Pepper and Gorgonzola Lasagna, 119

Index

Red Pepper Jelly, 19
Roasted Red Pepper Crostini, 28
Sautéed Artichoke Hearts with Red Bell Peppers, 188
Seafood Pepper Strips, 15
Tortellini with Peppers & Pine Nuts, 85

Peppy Pecans, 36

Persian Skewers, 164

Pesto
Angel Hair Pasta with Crab and Pesto, 105
Baked White Fish with Pesto, 132
Basil Pesto, 105
Cilantro Pesto Pasta, 111
Layered Tomato Pesto, 17
Orzo with Parmesan and Pesto, 183

Pheasant
Palouse Pheasant with Mushroom Sauce, 155

Phyllo-Wrapped Brie with Red Pepper Jelly, 19

Picnic Pizza Bread, 57

Pies
Blueberry Cream Pie, 213
No-Fail Pie Crust, 213
Northwest Huckleberry Pie, 214
Rhubarb Meringue Pie, 215
Vegetable Pie, 195

Pilaf-Style Couscous, 183

Pita Chips
Artichoke Relish with Pita Chips, 33

Pizza
Apple Streusel Pizza, 49
Fiery Thai Style Pizza, 153
Picnic Pizza Bread, 57
Pizza for Breakfast, 65
Premiere Pizza, 61

Pizza for Breakfast, 65

Popcorn
Almond Pecan Cashew Corn, 227

Popeye's Mostaccioli, 113

Pork
Cider Glazed Ham with Golden Delicious Apples, 172
Cranberry Pork Tenderloin, 174
Huckleberry Pork Chops, 177
Marinated Pork Tenderloin, 175
Oriental Glazed Spareribs, 177
Raspberry Grilled Pork Tenderloin with Salad, 173
Washington Pork Chops, 176

Potatoes
Celebration Potato Puffs, 186
Garlic Mashed Potatoes, 184

Herb Roasted Vegetables, 194
Herbed Potatoes in Parchment, 188
New Potato & Asparagus Salad, 92
New Potatoes with Herbed Shallot Butter, 185
New Potatoes and Leeks Dijon, 185
Smashing Potatoes, 184

Potatoes, Sweet
Light & Fluffy Sweet Potato Soufflé, 187

President's Cannelloni, 116

Premiere Pizza, 61

Pumpkin
Great Pumpkin Cookies, 223

Q
Quesadillas
Fontina Quesadillas, 34

Quick & Healthy Wheat Bread, 50

R
Raisin Oatmeal Bread, 50

Raspberries
Dark Chocolate Cheesecake with Raspberries and Cream, 210
Raspberry Grilled Pork Tenderloin with Salad, 173
Raspberry Kuchen, 47
Sumptuous Raspberry Spinach Salad, 91

Raspberry Grilled Pork Tenderloin with Salad, 173

Raspberry Kuchen, 47

Rave Reviews Dip, 31

Red Pepper and Gorgonzola Lasagna, 119

Red Pepper Jelly, 19

Rhubarb Meringue Pie, 215

Rice
Curried Pilaf with Corn, 181
Cypress Chicken and Rice, 143
Mexican Black Beans with Rice, 182
Pacific Fresh Wild Rice Salad, 82
Paradise Rice with Bean Sprouts, 181
Rice Pilaf with Mushrooms and Pecans, 182
Shrimp and St. Maries Wild Rice Soup, 74
Washington Wild Rice, 180
Wild Rice and Cranberry Pilaf, 180

Rice Pilaf with Mushrooms and Pecans, 182

Rick's Radio Roasted Chicken, 154

River Road Burritos with Avocado Salsa, 148

Roasted Red Pepper Crostini, 28

Robin's Chunky Chili, 167

Rolls
Cream Cheese Crescents, 45
Garlic Butter Buns, 56
Herb Rolls, 56

Romaine, Gorgonzola and Walnut Salad, 91

S
Salad Dressing
Buttermilk Bleu Salad Dressing, 100
Citrus Vinaigrette, 101
Honey Mustard Dressing, 101

Salads
Arugula and Goat Cheese Salad, 97
Asian Steak Salad, 80
Autumn Salad with Spicy Walnuts, 99
Baby Pea Salad with Cashews, 92
Bulgar Salad with Lemon and Curry, 86
Cashew Chicken Salad with Oranges, 88
Chutney Chicken Salad, 89
Crispy Crouton Salad, 87
Favorite Fruit, 93
Greek Orzo Salad with Shrimp, 83
Greens with Huckleberry Vinaigrette, 100
Huckleberry Drizzle Salad, 94
Incredible Couscous Salad, 84
Jicama Orange Salad, 95
Lemon Mint Chicken Salad, 90
New Potato & Asparagus Salad, 92
Pacific Fresh Wild Rice Salad, 82
Raspberry Grilled Pork Tenderloin with Salad, 173
Romaine, Gorgonzola and Walnut Salad, 91
Spicy Steak and Pasta Salad with Shiitake Mushrooms, 81
Spinach Salad with Papaya Salsa, 96
Springtime Salad, 93
Sumptuous Raspberry Spinach Salad, 91
The Ultimate Endive Salad, 98
Tortellini with Peppers & Pine Nuts, 85

Salads, Pasta
Greek Orzo Salad with Shrimp, 83
Incredible Couscous Salad, 84
Lemon Mint Chicken Salad, 90
Spicy Steak and Pasta Salad with Shiitake Mushrooms, 81
Tortellini with Peppers & Pine Nuts, 85

Salmon
Grilled Salmon with Yogurt Dill Sauce, 123
Salmon en Papillote, 122
Salmon in Phyllo, 124

INDEX

Salmon Tartlets, 13
Salmon with Ginger Butter, 125
Smoked Salmon with Apples, 12

Salmon en Papillote, 122

Salmon in Phyllo, 124

Salmon Tartlets, 13

Salmon with Ginger Butter, 125

Salsa
Black Bean Salsa, 29
Confetti Relish, 32
Mango Salsa, 136
Joanne's Spicy Shrimp Salsa, 28
Spinach Salad with Papaya Salsa, 96

Sandwich
Best Focaccia Beef Sandwich, 171
Muffuletta, 59
Southwestern Grilled Chicken Sandwiches, 149
Walla Walla Steak Sandwich with Horseradish Sauce, 170

Sauced Shrimp, 125

Sauces,
Basil Pesto, 105
Browned Butter Sauce, 107
Golden Tequila Sauce for White Fish, 133
Never Fail Hollandaise Sauce, 160
Quick Hollandaise Sauce, 160

Sausage, Italian
Italian Sausage and Bean Soup, 70
Italian Sausage Pasta, 114
Robin's Chunky Chili, 167
The King of Italian Meat Sauces, 115

Sautéed Artichoke Hearts with Red Bell Peppers, 188

Sautéed Mushrooms with Sherry, 189

Scallops
Bay Scallop Chowder, 73
Heavenly Marinara, 104
Scallops Fettuccine, 107
Scallops with Asparagus in Parchment, 132
Sun-Dried Scallop Sauté, 133

Scallops Fettuccine, 107

Scallops with Asparagus in Parchment, 132

Scampi Butter, 126

Scones
Cherry Scones, 46
Golden Raisin Scones, 47

Seafood Pepper Strips, 15

Seasoned Stuffed Sole, 135

Sensational Cauliflower, 197

Shrimp
Ginger Garlic Shrimp, 127
Glazed Shrimp Kabobs, 17
Greek Orzo Salad with Shrimp, 83
Indian Spiced Shrimp, 128
Joanne's Spicy Shrimp Salsa, 28
Pacific Fresh Cioppino, 130
Sauced Shrimp, 125
Shrimp and St. Maries Wild Rice Soup, 74
Shrimp and Tortellini Kabobs, 16
Shrimp in Phyllo, 126

Shrimp and St. Maries Wild Rice Soup, 74

Shrimp and Tortellini Kabobs, 16

Shrimp in Phyllo, 126

Smashing Potatoes, 184

Smoked Salmon with Apples, 12

Smoked Turkey in Endive, 26

Smothered Chicken, 142

Snapper
Caribbean Snapper, 131
Moroccan Fish, 131

Snowcapped Cookies, 221

Sole
Crab Stuffed Sole, 134
Seasoned Stuffed Sole, 135

Souffles
Chilled Amaretto Soufflé, 218
Light & Fluffy Sweet Potato Soufflé, 187
One at a Thyme Spinach Soufflés, 190

Soups, Cold
Chilled Corn Soup, 77
Cool Cucumber Soup, 76
Greenbluff Apple Soup, 77

Soups, Hot
Bay Scallop Chowder, 73
Carrot Soup with Coriander, 76
Italian Sausage and Bean Soup, 70
Kielbasa Cabbage Soup, 71
Mushroom Soup with Cashews, 74
Shrimp and St. Maries Wild Rice Soup, 74
Steptoe Butte Lentil Soup, 71
Thai Coconut Soup, 75
Thea's Bean Soup, 69
Tortellini Soup, 69
Tortilla Soup, 72
Tuscan Soup, 68

Sour Cream Sugar Cookies, 222

Southwestern Grilled Chicken Sandwiches, 149

Spicy Ginger Garlic Chicken, 151

Spicy Steak and Pasta Salad with Shiitake Mushrooms, 81

Spicy Summer Cucumbers, 201

Spinach
Baked Spinach Fettuccine, 110
Frosted Spinach Torte, 21
Italian Spinach Sauté, 191
One at a Thyme Spinach Soufflés, 190
Popeye's Mostaccioli, 113
Premiere Pizza, 61
Spinach and Feta Mushroom Caps, 22
Spinach Salad with Papaya Salsa, 96
Sumptuous Raspberry Spinach Salad, 91

Spinach and Feta Mushroom Caps, 22

Spinach Salad with Papaya Salsa, 96

Springtime Salad, 93

Steamed Clams with Sherry and Herbs, 18

Steptoe Butte Lentil Soup, 71

Stews
Black Bean and Turkey Stew, 156
Brandied Beef Stew, 168

Strawberries
Springtime Salad, 93

Sumptuous Raspberry Spinach Salad, 91

Sun-Dried Scallop Sauté, 133

Surprise Packages, 220

Swiss Cheese Breakfast Bake, 63

Swiss Onion Bread Ring, 55

T

Tantalizing Toffee Squares, 226

Tarts
Chocolate Macadamia Tart, 216

Tenderloin Deluxe, 161

Thai Chicken Fettuccine, 108

Thai Coconut Soup, 75

The Great Turkey Caper, 157

The King of Italian Meat Sauces, 115

The Ultimate Endive Salad, 98

Thea's Bean Soup, 69

Tortellini Primavera, 112

Tortellini Soup, 69

INDEX

Tortellini with Peppers & Pine Nuts, 85

Tortes
    Coconut Pecan Torte, 217
    Frosted Spinach Torte, 21

Tortilla Soup, 72

Trout
    Catch & Keep Grilled Trout, 129

Turkey
    Black Bean and Turkey Stew, 156
    The Great Turkey Caper, 157
    Incredible Couscous Salad, 84
    Smoked Turkey in Endive, 26
    Turkey Tidbits, 157

Turkey Tidbits, 157

Tuscan Soup, 68

Two Pepper Steak, 165

V

Valentine Cake, 205

Vegetable Pie, 195

Vegetarian Entrees
    Baked Spinach Fettuccine, 110
    Basil Mushroom Fettuccine with Tomato, 110
    Browned Butter Sauce, 107
    Cilantro Pesto Pasta, 111
    Mama B's Baked Ziti, 117
    Mexican Black Beans with Rice, 182
    Popeye's Mostaccioli, 113
    President's Cannelloni, 116
    Red Pepper and Gorgonzola Lasagna, 119
    Thea's Bean Soup, 69
    Tortellini Primavera, 112
    Vegetable Pie, 195

W

Walla Walla Sweet Squares, 20

Walla Walla Steak Sandwich with
    Horseradish Sauce, 170

Walnuts
    Autumn Salad with Spicy Walnuts, 99
    Romaine, Gorgonzola and Walnut Salad, 91

Washington Pork Chops, 176

Washington Wild Rice, 180

Wild Rice
    Pacific Fresh Wild Rice Salad, 82
    Shrimp and St. Maries Wild Rice Soup, 74
    Washington Wild Rice, 180
    Wild Rice and Cranberry Pilaf, 180

Z

Zucchini
    Herb Roasted Vegetables, 194
    Mediterranean Skewers, 23
    One Hundred and One Zucchini, 193
    Zucchini & Feta Fantastic, 193

Zucchini & Feta Fantastic, 193

ORDER FORM

Please send **Gold'n Delicious** to:

Name: _____

Address: _____

City, State, Zip _____

Phone ( ) _____

_____ COOKBOOKS   X $22.95 $_____

(WA addresses add 8% sales tax) $_____

SHIPPING & HANDLING
    per book $3.00 $_____

TOTAL ENCLOSED $_____

MAKE CHECKS PAYABLE AND SEND ORDER TO:

Junior League of Spokane
910 North Washington, Suite 228
Spokane, WA 99201-2260

FAX ORDERS: (509) 328-1827
PHONE ORDERS: (509) 328-2166

OR CHARGE TO:

_____ VISA   _____ MASTERCARD

Account Number: _____

Expiration Date: _____

Signature of Cardholder: _____